THIS BOOK MIGHT BLOW YOUR MIND

by
Cheryl Blackford, Connie Colwell Miller,
Megan Cooley Peterson, Christopher Forest,
Danielle S. Hammelef, Hans Hetrick,
Karen M. Leet and Kristi Lew

A COLLECTION OF AWESOME TRIVIA

UNUSUAL WEATHER

GROSS FACTS

STRANGE SCIENCE

MILITARY DETAILS

WACKY ANIMALS

AMERICAN HISTORY

ODD ODDS

AWESOME SPORTS

CAPSTONE PRESS
a capstone imprint

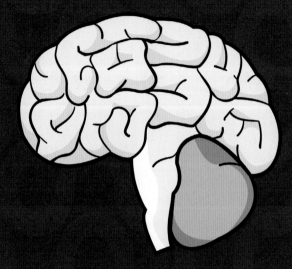

Capstone Press,
1710 Roe Crest Drive, North Mankato, Minnesota 56003.
www.capstonepub.com

Library of Congress Cataloging-in-Publication Data
Cataloging-in-publication information is on file with the Library of Congress.
ISBN 978-1-4765-7746-3

Printed in the United States of America in Stevens Point, Wisconsin.
072013   007635R

TABLE OF CONTENTS

CHAPTER ONE

STARTLING ODDS TRIVIA

WHAT ARE THE ODDS?

Have you ever heard someone ask, "What are the odds?" What do people mean when they say this? Odds are a way of stating how likely or unlikely it is that something will happen.

As the difference between the numbers gets bigger, events become less likely to happen. Let's say that you would like to get a new pet. You might really want to get a pet elephant. But the odds of your parents agreeing to a pet elephant are 1 in 1 million. The odds against getting an elephant are pretty huge. However, the odds of getting a pet dog are just 1 in 3. You have a much better chance of getting a dog than an elephant!

Odds can be used for everything. Some are funny or weird. Some may surprise you. And some may even have happened to you!

BIZARRE BODIES

Some people are born with extra body parts or incredible intelligence. Sometimes people get hurt in strange or unexpected ways. Do you know anyone who has experienced these unusual conditions?

What if you wanted a banana but couldn't tell if it was green or yellow? People who are color-blind see the world in shades of gray. The chances of being born color-blind are 1 in 30,000. More boys than girls are color-blind.

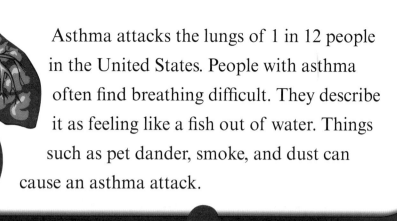

Asthma attacks the lungs of 1 in 12 people in the United States. People with asthma often find breathing difficult. They describe it as feeling like a fish out of water. Things such as pet dander, smoke, and dust can cause an asthma attack.

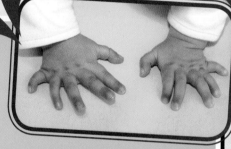

If babies could count, some could count to 11 or 12 on their fingers. One out of every 1,000 babies is born with extra fingers. These extra fingers usually form next to a person's pinkie finger. The extra fingers can be well formed with their own bones, or they can be extra skin. Doctors usually operate to remove them.

Doctors sometimes seem like miracle workers. But they can make mistakes like anyone else. Sometimes surgery patients wake up with surgical tools still inside their bodies! These tools have included sponges, needles, clamps, and scalpels. The odds of a doctor making this medical mistake during a surgery are 1 in 7,000.

Do you know anyone who can bend his or her thumb backward to the wrist? Maybe you have seen people put their legs behind their heads. People who can do these things are double-jointed. The odds of someone being double-jointed are 1 in 10.

You may have to share your toys, a TV, or even your bedroom with a brother or sister. But imagine if you had to share body parts! The odds of being a conjoined twin are 1 in 50,000. Most conjoined twins are connected at the chest. The twins may share body parts such as a heart. Doctors can separate the babies if each has all the body parts needed to live.

People often celebrate Independence Day with fireworks. But sometimes "Oohs!" and "Ahhs!" turn to "Owws!" Every year some people in the United States suffer injuries on the Fourth of July. The chances of getting hurt from handling fireworks are about 1 in 20,000.

During the first weeks of pregnancy, a baby's hands and feet resemble flat paddles. As the baby grows, the paddles separate into fingers and toes. However, sometimes the fingers and toes stay connected by skin or bone. The odds that a baby's fingers or toes will remain joined together are 1 in 2,500. This condition occurs most often between the middle and ring fingers. Boys are twice as likely as girls to have joined fingers or toes.

Shampoo commercials often show people washing their thick hair. But what if you didn't have any hair anywhere on your body? Alopecia (al-oh-PEE-shah) is a disease in which people's bodies attack their hair. The hair falls out and may never grow back. People around the world have about a 1 in 50 chance of having this condition.

Sometimes people use an intelligence quotient (IQ) test to learn how smart they are. People with IQs greater than 135 are considered geniuses. Famous geniuses include Albert Einstein and Wolfgang Amadeus Mozart. Einstein had an IQ of 160, while Mozart's was 165. Just 1 in 50 people in the world have the IQ of a genius.

Now that's a ton of dirty diapers! Quadruplets, or four babies born at the same time, are rare. In the United States, the odds of being born a quadruplet are 1 in 700,000. In 2009, 355 U.S. moms gave birth to quadruplets.

Have you ever seen an all-white animal with red or blue eyes? These animals are called albinos. The skin, hair, and eyes all lack normal color. The odds of a wild animal being born an albino are 1 in 10,000. People can be albinos too. The worldwide odds of a person being born an albino are 1 in 20,000.

Are you one of the 1 in 7 people who sleepwalk? When people sleepwalk, they may have their eyes open. They may walk around inside the house or out the front door. People have even driven cars while sleepwalking!

WHAT'S FOR DINNER?

What's for dinner? For some people, the answer to that question is important. They may have food allergies, or they might get an upset stomach from some foods. What are the odds that you and your food won't get along?

Is your food safe to eat? You can't always tell if food is spoiled just by looking at it. Some chemicals and bacteria can make food dangerous to eat. Signs of food poisoning include an upset stomach, fever, diarrhea, and vomiting. In the United States, the odds of getting sick from food poisoning during the year are 1 in 6.

Peanuts are nuts only in name. Peanuts are really legumes like peas or beans. But these tasty little snacks can cause big problems for people with peanut allergies. Symptoms can include stomach cramps, wheezing, swelling, vomiting, diarrhea, and hives. The odds of having a peanut allergy are 1 in 100.

What if you couldn't tell the difference between your favorite food and cardboard? Or worse, what if your taste buds failed to warn you that your milk had spoiled? Some people develop taste problems after an injury or illness. The odds of having reduced or complete loss of taste are 1 in 15.

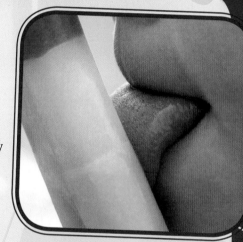

Did you know that millions of people actually say, "No thanks!" to ice cream? Dairy products like milk and ice cream contain lactose. Seven out of 10 people in the world can't digest lactose. When they eat or drink dairy products, they may suffer stomach cramps, diarrhea, gas, and bloating.

The odds of being born with diabetes are 1 in 12. Diabetes is a disease in which a person's body can't process sugar properly. Too much sugar in the blood can cause major health problems for these people. Uncontrolled diabetes can lead to kidney failure, blindness, and the loss of toes, feet, or legs.

In the United States, the odds are 1 in 31 that a person is a vegetarian. Some of these people choose to eat only plants to help improve their health. Others believe being a vegetarian can save animals and help the environment.

Can you smell "asparagus pee?" When a person's body digests asparagus, it produces a chemical that smells like rotten eggs. This stinky chemical exits your body as waste in your urine. The chemical drifts up to your nose when you pee. Everyone's pee reeks after eating asparagus, but only 1 in 4 people can smell it.

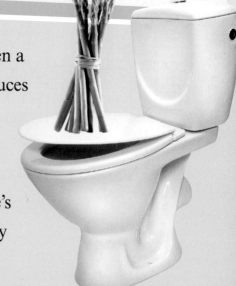

When you eat ice cream too fast, the odds that you'll get brain freeze from it are 1 in 3. The blood vessels in the roof of your mouth tend to shrink quickly when cold foods touch them. Your body senses this and quickly sends more blood to your head. The extra blood causes your head to pound and hurt. People often call this effect brain freeze. The pain usually goes away after a minute.

WHEN NATURE ATTACKS

People have walked on the moon and cured life-threatening diseases. But in spite of many high-tech advances, people still can't control nature. Natural disasters hit without warning, and animal attacks happen when we least expect them. When nature strikes, what are the odds someone will feel its power?

In movies sharks are often shown as man-eating monsters. Sharks do occasionally bite people. But attacks are rare. Millions of people visit ocean beaches each year, but sharks attack only a few people. The odds of being bitten by a shark are only 1 in 11.5 million.

Odds are 3 in 4 that any given tornado will touch down in the United States. Tornadoes can touch down anywhere in the world. Approximately 1,500 tornadoes are reported worldwide each year. About 1,125 of those tornadoes occur in the United States.

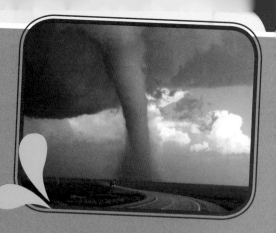

Tsunamis are like powerful trains of large ocean waves. Underwater earthquakes and volcanic eruptions often cause tsunamis. These monster waves can travel more than 500 miles (800 km) per hour. In any given year, the odds that a tsunami will hit the eastern coast of North America are 1 in 1,000. Odds on the western coast are much higher—up to 1 in 2.2.

The odds of being struck by lightning range from 1 in 500,000 to 1 in 1 million. Those are very low odds for most people—unless you are Roy Sullivan. The Virginia park ranger was struck by lightning seven different times and lived to tell about it!

Avalanches can race down mountainsides at 80 miles (129 km) per hour. If caught in an avalanche, your survival chances depend on how long you're buried. Odds are 9 in 10 if someone digs you out within 15 minutes. But the odds decrease to 1 in 2 if you are buried for 30 minutes. If you are buried for 45 minutes, your odds drop to 1 in 5. After two hours, the chances of survival for most people are zero.

Lice are parasites the size of sesame seeds. They can live about 30 days on your scalp and lay up to 150 eggs. If your head is constantly itchy, you may have lice. These tiny bloodsuckers are a common problem for millions of people. Each year about 1 in 5 children in the United States suffer from lice.

Bees, wasps, yellow jackets, and hornets sting to defend themselves. The odds of children having a severe allergic reaction from a bee sting are 1 in 100. Major reactions include difficulty breathing, dizziness, and difficulty swallowing.

Asteroids are large rocks that circle the sun. They range in size from 20 feet (6 meters) to 580 miles (933 km) wide. If a large asteroid hit Earth, life could be wiped out. But don't worry. The odds of a big asteroid hitting Earth are just 1 in 100 million.

In the United States, most earthquakes occur in the northwest. The odds of a major earthquake hitting the northwest are 1 in 3. The central states have lower odds of 1 in 10. The odds for the eastern states are even lower—just 1 in 67.

WHAT ARE YOU AFRAID OF?

Your heart beats faster and faster. Your stomach feels like it's full of spiders. Sweat soaks your skin. Are you sick? Maybe. But you may be feeling a strong fear called a phobia. Read on to learn the odds of being afraid of creepy-crawlies, heights, and more.

Does looking over the edge of a cliff scare you? How about climbing a ladder or walking across a narrow bridge? If you answered yes, you may have a fear of heights called acrophobia. This fear is a common condition. The odds of having acrophobia are 1 in 3.

Aviophobia is the fear of flying. This fear keeps many people from getting on an airplane. Some people feel scared when high off the ground with nothing under the plane. Others worry about being in a crash. The odds of having aviophobia are 1 in 3.

Slithering, scaly snakes and lizards scare a lot of people. Many stories show snakes as evil creatures with dangerous, venomous bites. The odds are 1 in 2 that you will have a fear of snakes and other reptiles, or herpetophobia.

A fear of the dark is called nyctophobia. Makers of horror films create scary scenes that play on this fear. Many people are scared of not knowing what or who may be hiding in the dark.

Others fear getting lost or hurt if they can't see. People have a 1 in 20 chance of having nyctophobia.

Eeek! Spiders make some people squirm. People with arachnophobia may be afraid of being bitten by a spider. They might fear getting sick. Or perhaps they just think these creatures are ugly. The odds of having this phobia are 1 in 4.

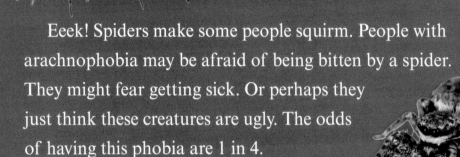

Small spaces make people with claustrophobia feel trapped. The walls seem to close in tighter by the second. Claustrophobic people often don't like shower stalls or elevators. They may refuse to use sleeping bags or wear tight clothes. The odds of having claustrophobia are 1 in 3.

Dogs are popular pets for millions of people. But if a dog growls, chases, or bites someone, that person may become afraid of all dogs. This condition is called cynophobia. Most people with this phobia develop it after being attacked by a dog. Odds of having a fear of dogs are 1 in 9.

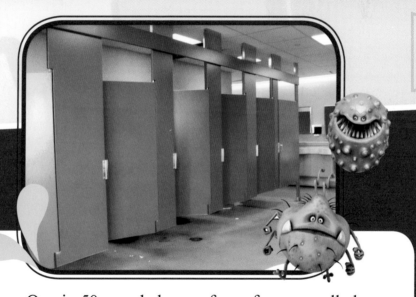

One in 50 people have a fear of germs called mysophobia. Since germs live everywhere, these people think they will easily get sick. People with this fear avoid places they think have too many germs, such as public bathrooms.

A woman is cooking dinner when a mouse skitters across the counter. She screams and throws her cooking spoon at the mouse. She has musophobia, or a fear of mice. Some people fear getting bitten by the small rodents. Others fear finding mouse poop in their food. The odds of someone having musophobia are 1 in 5.

Although doctors work hard to save people's lives, 1 in 11 people fear going to the doctor. Iatrophobia (EYE-a-troh-foh-bee-uh) keeps people from visiting the doctor, even if they're sick. Some may not like being examined by the doctor. Other people worry the doctor will give them bad news about their health.

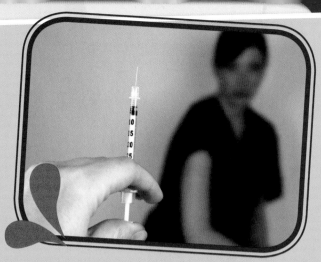

Nobody looks forward to getting a shot at the doctor's office. But some people fear getting a shot so much that they faint. Some might even run away. A few may even run away when they see someone else getting a shot. Odds of having trypanophobia (trip-AN-oh-foh-bee-uh), or a fear of needles or shots, are 1 in 5.

People with glossophobia usually avoid speaking in public. This fear affects 2 in 5 people. Those with this condition might feel like millions of eyes are watching them—just waiting for them to make a mistake.

GIVE ME A SPORTING CHANCE

Sports offer everyone the chance to beat the odds. For some people this means reaching the top of the world. For others it means slamming a game-winning home run. Keep reading to learn about beating the odds in some of your favorite sports.

Each year sees the three biggest events in horse racing—the Kentucky Derby, the Preakness, and the Belmont Stakes. If a horse wins all three races, it is considered a Triple Crown winner. There is only a 1 in 247 chance of a horse winning all three races. In 136 years only 11 horses have captured the Triple Crown. The last horse to win it was Affirmed in 1978.

Odds that a professional golfer can make a hole-in-one shot are 1 to 3,000. Average golfers have only a 1 in 12,000 chance. The longest hole in one measured 448 yards (410 m), which is almost as long as four football fields!

Strike! The best bowlers want to hear that cheer 12 times in one game. When they do, they have beaten the odds of bowling a perfect game. The odds of getting all strikes and scoring 300 points in one game are 1 in 11,500.

In Major League Baseball (MLB), players "hit for the cycle" in about 1 out of every 800 games. A player hits for the cycle when he hits a single, double, triple, and home run during one game. Natural cycles are even more rare. A player gets a natural cycle when he gets those hits in order. Only 14 players have hit natural cycles in major-league history.

Olympic athletes compete for bronze, silver, and gold medals every four years. The odds of winning an Olympic medal are 1 in 660,000. U.S. Olympic swimmer Michael Phelps has beaten the odds 22 times. In 2004 he won six gold medals and two bronze medals. In 2008 he won eight golds. In 2012 he won four golds and two silvers.

The odds that a mountain climber will reach the top of the tallest mountain on Earth are 1 in 5. Mount Everest towers 29,035 feet (8,850 m) above sea level. Climbers on Everest brave hurricane-force winds up to 175 miles (282 km) per hour. Temperatures often drop below -25 degrees Fahrenheit (-32 degrees Celsius). In 2010 Jordan Romero became the youngest person to beat the odds of climbing Everest. He reached the top of the world at age 13.

Take me out to the ball game! Millions of fans attend major-league baseball games every season. Some bring their mitts hoping to catch a home run or a foul ball hit into the stands. The odds of a fan catching a ball at a baseball game during the season are 1 in 563.

Have you ever dreamed of being a professional athlete? Many people dream of getting paid to play sports. But the odds of this dream coming true are low—just 1 in 22,000.

EVERYDAY ODDS

Odds are everywhere and affect everything we do. We make decisions based on odds every day. For example, let's say your parents are planning to make either pizza or meatloaf for dinner. There is a 50 percent chance of having either pizza or meatloaf. The odds of getting pizza are 1 in 2. Knowing this, will you fill up on snacks before dinner or save room for pizza? See if you can improve your odds of getting pizza for dinner by impressing your parents with your new knowledge about odds!

CHAPTER TWO

WACKY ANIMAL TRIVIA

STRANGE BUT TRUE

A hairy-looking frog. A bug that hears with its knees. A snail that blows bubbles. These animals aren't creatures from a horror movie. They're all real.

Some animal bodies, behaviors, and homes might seem odd to us. But animals have adapted to live in their habitats. They have unique ways of finding food and staying safe. Animals keep what works and change what doesn't.

Certain animals look and act so strange that they might seem unbelievable. But when it comes to animals, sometimes truth is stranger than fiction! Get ready to meet some real freaks of nature.

WHAT'S FOR LUNCH?

Animals whip up all sorts of meals. But their idea of a tasty meal is probably different than yours. You might not want to eat after reading about some strange animal cuisine.

You wouldn't want to invite a vampire bat to lunch. Not only do vampire bats drink animal blood, they pee while they eat! These bats lap up half their body weight in blood each night. Peeing helps them lose weight so they can fly away.

Aardvarks gobble up to 50,000 termites and ants in a single night.

Rabbits enjoy their food so much they eat it twice. They have two kinds of droppings—hard, brown feces and soft balls filled with important nutrients. The soft droppings are coated with mucus so they aren't digested. Rabbits eat them to get nutrients from plants that are hard to digest.

Meat cookie, anyone? Cookiecutter sharks feast on tuna, swordfish, whales, and dolphins. But they don't just take a bite and swim away. These sharks sink sharp teeth into their victims and spin in a circle. Then they suck out a "cookie" of flesh.

Some honeypot ants become so fat with stored honeydew they can no longer walk. Instead they hang upside down inside the nest to serve as living food containers. Other ants eat their vomit.

Jackals don't waste their food. They eat dead animal flesh and feed their young by vomiting. If the young can't finish their food, the adults eat their own puke.

Cows eat a high-fiber diet of grass, which causes them to burp and fart almost constantly. In the United States, cows release 6 million tons (5.4 million metric tons) of methane gas each year.

Baby koalas eat their mothers' soupy poop. The special poop is called pap. It is filled with important microorganisms. The microorganisms prepare the young koalas' digestive systems for a diet of toxin-filled eucalyptus leaves.

Humpback whales can reach lengths of more than 60 feet (18 m). They have appetites as big as their bodies. These whales often hunt in groups. They surround schools of fish with air bubbles. The bubbles trap the fish like a net. The whales then swim through the net to feast on the fish buffet.

The tiger shark didn't earn the nickname "wastebasket of the sea" for nothing. License plates, tires, fast-food wrappers, and even a set of antlers have been found inside tiger sharks' stomachs.

Honey might be tasty, but the way honeybees make it is anything but sweet. First, worker bees store nectar in their honey stomachs, which break down the nectar's sugars. Back at the hive, they vomit the nectar. The water evaporates, and the bee barf becomes honey.

Candiru catfish get attached to their food. These tiny fish live in the Amazon River. Candiru catfish swim into the gills of larger fish and latch on with hooks located on their heads. Then they suck up blood for 30 seconds to three minutes.

Watch Where You Pee

Fish gills aren't the only places candiru catfish swim into. In 1997 a man swimming in the Amazon River decided to pee in it. A few days later, doctors found a dead candiru catfish lodged in his urethra. Scientists believe the candiru may have confused the man's urine with chemicals that larger fish leave behind. The fish then followed the urine to its source. Although the candiru rarely latches on to humans, you probably wouldn't want to pee in the Amazon River!

OUTRAGEOUS WACKY ANIMAL TRIVIA

HOME SWEET HOME

Animals, like people, need places to live. Some of these homes are just plain weird. Check out some of the oddest places animals call home.

African termites build nests that look like skyscrapers. They build these nests out of clay and spit. A single nest can rise more than 25 feet (7.6 m) above the ground. That's taller than the average adult male giraffe!

We should have built an elevator.

The world's largest badger burrow ever found contained 2,883 feet (879 m) of underground tunnels. The burrow had 50 rooms and 178 entrances.

The edible-nest swiftlets of Asia build their nests almost entirely out of spit. The male birds attach spit strings to rock walls, and the spit hardens. What's more surprising? Some people in Asia use the nests to make bird's nest soup.

Burying beetles build disgusting homes for their young. They bury dead animals, such as birds and mice. The females lay their eggs near the bodies. When the young hatch, they have a "fresh" supply of rotting meat to feast on.

Not all ants call underground nests home. Weaver ants build nests out of leaves and silk. First, worker ants pull two leaves together. Others glue them together using silk from larvae. They move the larvae back and forth like tiny sewing machines.

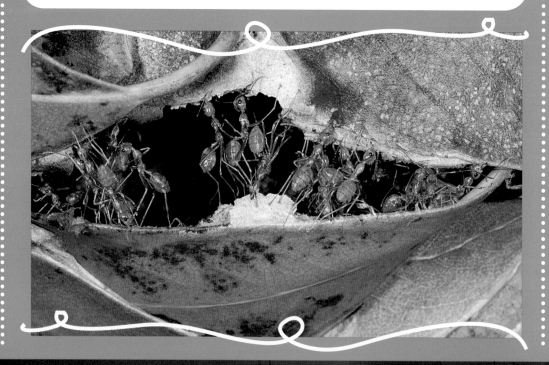

Have you ever blown a spit bubble? Now imagine living on it! Violet sea snails live in the ocean but can't swim. They build rafts out of mucus bubbles that float on the water's surface. The snails hang upside down from the bubbles their entire lives. If the rafts break, the snails drown.

Old houses and dark basements aren't the only places creepy, crawly spiders call home. European water spiders spend most of their lives in water but breathe air. These spiders spin bell-shaped silk nests underwater. Then they fill the nests with air bubbles.

The world's largest beaver dam was discovered in Canada in 2007. It was about 2,800 feet (850 m) long. That's as long as eight football fields!

AMAZING BODIES

Some animals might look like they're dressed up in Halloween costumes. But their odd-looking bodies help them find food, stay safe, and fight off enemies. Learn about some of nature's most amazing animal bodies.

Can you imagine large, glowing green eyes staring out at you from inside a see-through head? The Pacific barreleye fish has tube-shaped eyes that are visible through its head. Tubular eyes collect more light in deep waters. A see-through head protects the fish's eyes from the stings of deep-sea jellyfish.

The star-nosed mole has 22 pink tentacles on its nose. It uses them to identify food by touch. Star-nosed moles can find, identify, and eat an insect in less than one second.

The blue whale is the world's largest animal. Its heart weighs as much as a small car. Its tongue is the size of an adult elephant.

The next time you hear someone say he's "sweating like a pig," share this fact—pigs don't sweat! Because they don't have sweat glands, pigs relax in mud to keep cool.

To blend in with the ocean floor, flatfish spend their entire adult lives lying on their sides. They have eyes on only one side of their heads. At birth, they look like regular fish until one eye moves to the opposite side of the head.

A cricket's ears are located in each of its front legs below the knees.

The tuatara is a reptile with a third eye on top of its head. The eye has a lens and a retina. It's connected to the brain by a nerve. Although scales cover the eye, it is sensitive to light and may help the tuatara control body temperature. Other reptiles have less-developed third eyes.

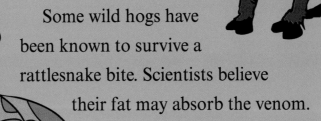

Some wild hogs have been known to survive a rattlesnake bite. Scientists believe their fat may absorb the venom.

If rats and mice give you the creeps, you wouldn't want to meet a capybara. The capybara is the world's largest rodent. Found in Central and South America, it can weigh more than 100 pounds (45 kilograms).

The skin of a wild golden poison dart frog can contain enough venom to kill 20,000 mice or 10 adult humans. Just holding one of these deadly frogs may kill you.

An African elephant's trunk contains about 100,000 muscles. The human body has between 650 and 850 muscles. Elephants use their trunks to breathe, eat, drink, and pick up objects.

Tarsiers are small animals with huge eyes. In fact, each eye is as big as its brain! Tarsiers are nocturnal, and large eyes help them see well at night. Since they can't move their eyes, tarsiers rotate their heads like owls.

Some scientists believe Tyrannosaurus rex's closest living relative may be the chicken. They claim that proteins found in a 68-million-year-old T-rex bone closely match those found in chickens.

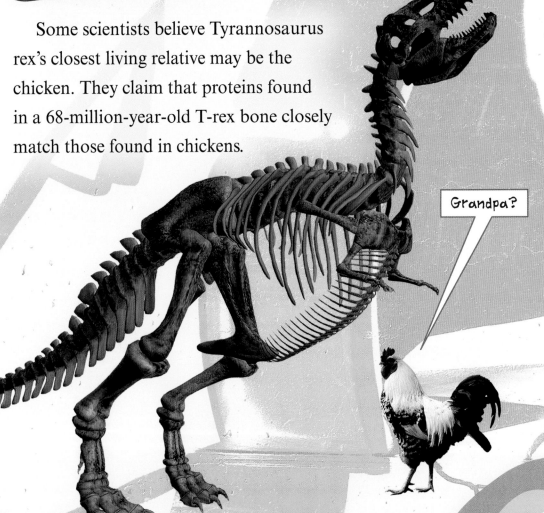

Grandpa?

People once believed that hippopotamuses sweated blood. But the oily, red substance that oozes from their skin is really a built-in sunscreen.

Delicious!

Female butterflies test out food for their young. They taste plants with their feet to make sure they're safe for caterpillars to feed on.

A polar bear's fur is clear, which allows sunlight to pass through it. Light bouncing off the fur makes it look white. Black skin under the fur absorbs the sun's warmth.

Male African hairy frogs grow long, hairlike strands of skin from their bodies during mating season. The "hairs" help the frogs breathe through their skin as they sit on eggs underwater.

Scorpions glow under ultraviolet lights. Proteins in their exoskeleton make them fluorescent. Scientists aren't sure why they glow.

One Tough Bug

Scorpions are able to survive harsh conditions. Their bodies slow the process of changing food into energy. They can live for a year after eating only one insect. One scientist even froze scorpions. The next day, the scorpions thawed in the sun and walked away.

BIZARRE BEHAVIOR

People can't spit up slime or walk around without heads. But in the animal kingdom, odd behavior is normal. Get ready to meet some animals whose bizarre behavior will leave you scratching your head.

Off with his head!

Hey—not so fast!

A cockroach can still cause some trouble after losing its head. A headless cockroach can walk around for weeks. The cockroach's brain isn't needed for breathing. But without a mouth, it eventually starves to death.

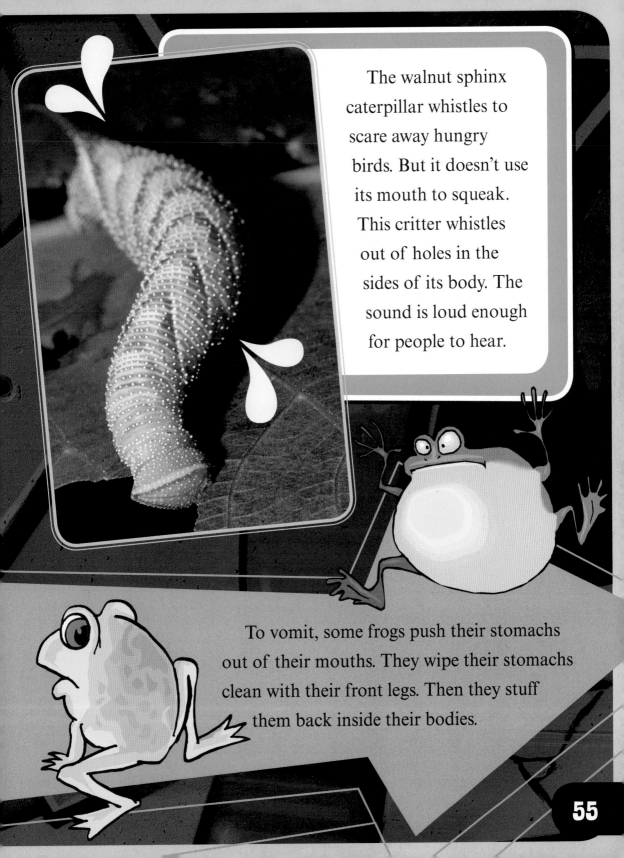

The walnut sphinx caterpillar whistles to scare away hungry birds. But it doesn't use its mouth to squeak. This critter whistles out of holes in the sides of its body. The sound is loud enough for people to hear.

To vomit, some frogs push their stomachs out of their mouths. They wipe their stomachs clean with their front legs. Then they stuff them back inside their bodies.

Humans sweat to cool off. But what if you didn't have any sweat glands? Some vultures and storks have a disgusting way of keeping cool—they pee and poop on their legs. As the liquid in their waste evaporates, it cools the blood.

Move over, great white shark. The trap-jaw ant has the fastest bite on Earth. It snaps its jaws shut at up to 145 miles (233 km) per hour. It can chomp down on prey in less than a millisecond.

The pistol shrimp makes a sound like a gunshot by snapping shut its oversized claw. As the claw closes, a jet of bubbles shoots out. The bubbles break and create a shock wave that stuns the pistol shrimp's prey.

Malaysian carpenter ants are walking bombs. The worker ants violently tighten their muscles when threatened. This action causes poison glands inside their bodies to explode. They die protecting the ant colony.

Watch out for flying body parts! When alarmed, some sea cucumbers will blow sticky threads or even internal organs out of their backsides. Startled predators give sea cucumbers time to escape. Sea cucumbers can then regrow these body parts.

Come on, follow me!

Farting in public might seem like bad manners. But herring communicate by passing gas. These fish gulp air and pass it out their backsides to "talk" to one another when it's dark.

Sand tiger sharks are vicious even before they are born. Females carry several pups, but only two are actually born. The developing sharks eat their brothers and sisters until only two remain.

The West Indian wood snake is a master at playing dead. It gives off the smell of rotting flesh and fills its eyes with blood. Blood even oozes from its mouth. Predators pass up this snake for more appealing snacks.

Owls don't make a sound as they swoop toward prey. The feathers on the back ends of their wings reduce noise. Down feathers on the legs and body absorb the rest of the sound. Flight engineers study owl feathers to make quieter airplanes.

SEEING IS BELIEVING

From living in poop to building giant homes, animals amaze us with their unique homes, bodies, and behaviors. When it comes to animal oddities, sometimes you have to see them to believe them!

CHAPTER THREE

BIZARRE
SCIENCE
TRIVIA

WACKY WORLD OF SCIENCE

➡ You had more bones when you were born than you do now.

➡ Astronauts get taller in space.

➡ Table salt is formed by a reaction between a metal and a poisonous gas.

These pieces of information may sound like science fiction, but they're really science fact. Let's explore the explanations for these facts and many others. Welcome to the wonderful, wild, wacky world of science!

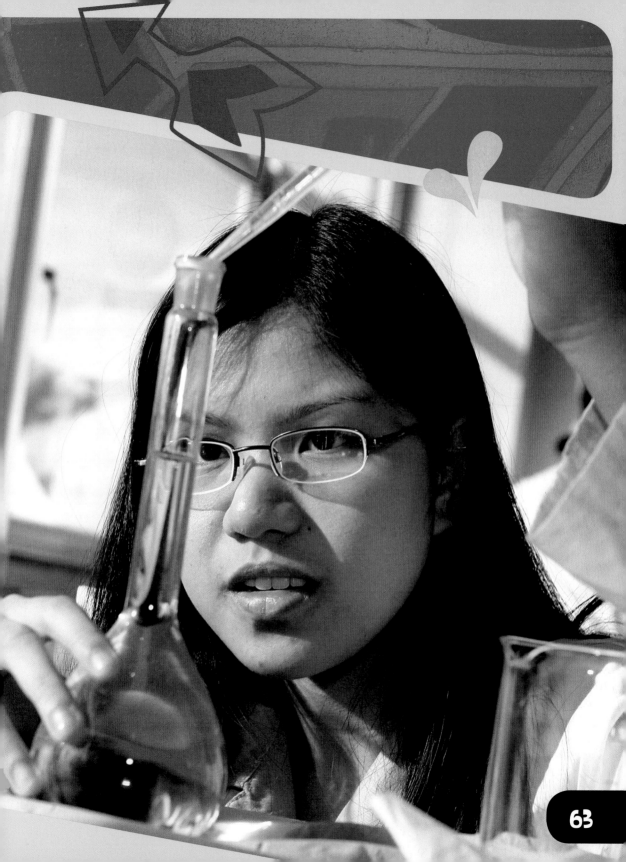

EXTREME EARTH

Earth can be a pretty strange place. Think all deserts are hot? Think again. Let's explore wild facts about our amazing planet.

You know that ocean water contains salt, right? But did you know that if all the salt in the ocean was removed and spread evenly over Earth's land surface, it would be more than 500 feet (152 m) thick? That's about the height of a 50-story building!

Have you ever heard someone say, "that will knock your socks off"? A lightning strike can actually knock a person's shoes and socks off! As lightning travels across the body's surface, damp skin in the path of the current produces high-pressure steam. This can knock off shoes and socks!

It's easy to float in the Dead Sea—people just bob on top of the water like a cork. Water in the Dead Sea has about six times more salt in it than any other saltwater body of water. All this salt makes the water denser than the human body, allowing you to float freely.

The Cave of Swallows in San Luis Potosi, Mexico, is deep enough to hold the 102-story Empire State Building. With a vertical drop of 1,220 feet (372 m), this cave is one of the deepest on Earth. In fact, it is so deep that explorers sometimes parachute to the bottom!

65

Not all deserts are hot. Freezing cold Antarctica is Earth's largest desert. Deserts get less than 10 inches (25 cm) of precipitation a year. Antarctica averages about 2 inches (5 cm) of snowfall a year. This makes the cold continent drier than the blazing hot Sahara Desert, which gets 3 inches (7.6 cm) of rain each year.

People spend about a quarter of their lives growing. But did you know that mountains also grow? Mount Everest is the world's tallest mountain. It is getting taller every year! Earth's crust is broken into chunks called plates. These plates slowly move and crash into each other. These collisions push Mount Everest upward by about 0.2 inch (5 mm) a year.

I'll be taller next year!

Volcanoes often form slowly. But one was in a hurry to grow up! On February 20, 1943, the ground opened near the village of Paricutin, Mexico. Hot rocks shot from the opening. By the end of the day, the new volcano was 35 feet (11 m) high. By 1952 it measured 1,391 feet (424 m) and had destroyed two towns.

Did you know waterfalls flow beneath the sea? These waterfalls are called cataracts. The largest cataract is between Greenland and Iceland. It drops nearly 11,500 feet (3,505 m). This is more than three times the length of Angel Falls in Venezuela, Earth's highest above-ground waterfall.

Angel Falls ⭐

Ocean waves need wind or storms to develop, right? Not so fast. Rogue waves up to 100 feet (30 m) tall can form in calm water. These waves form when several smaller waves come together at the same moment.

If you've ever been around a natural gas leak, you've probably held your nose. The gas smells like rotten eggs! But natural gas really has no odor. Leaking natural gas explodes very easily. Gas companies add chemicals to make the gas smell bad. People then recognize the odor and get to safety.

GAS

GAS

What makes the White Cliffs of Dover, England, so white? Chalk! Chalk is made up of skeletons of trillions of plankton. As the plankton died, they settled to the bottom of the ocean. Heat and pressure turned the layers of skeletons into rock. Movements of Earth's plates shoved the rock upward, making it dry land.

Lightning strikes the Earth more than 8 million times a day. The air around a lightning bolt can be as hot as 50,000 degrees Fahrenheit (27,760 degrees Celsius). Southwestern Florida has an average of 100 days with thunderstorms each year. This makes it the U.S. lightning capital!

CRAZY CHEMISTRY

Did you know that every day you eat a chemical made from an exploding metal and a poisonous gas? Or that regular household vinegar could destroy your mother's favorite pearl necklace? Keep reading to learn how all this crazy chemistry works.

The ocean is filled with trace elements of gold. If all of that gold was removed from the ocean, every person on Earth could receive 9 pounds (4 kg) of the precious metal!

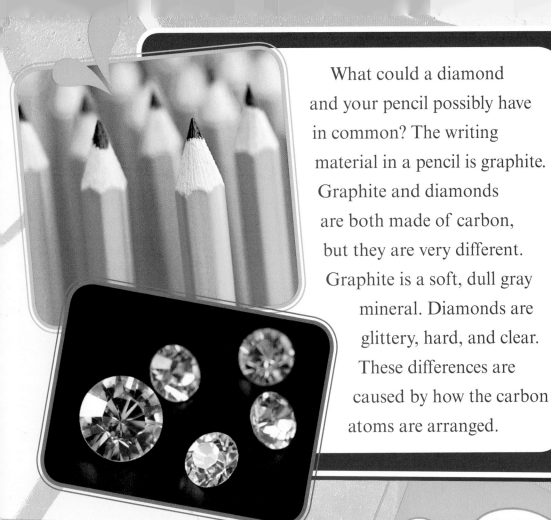

What could a diamond and your pencil possibly have in common? The writing material in a pencil is graphite. Graphite and diamonds are both made of carbon, but they are very different. Graphite is a soft, dull gray mineral. Diamonds are glittery, hard, and clear. These differences are caused by how the carbon atoms are arranged.

Most metals are hard and cool to the touch. But the metal mercury is liquid at room temperature and standard atmospheric pressure. Mercury was once used in thermometers to measure temperature. Now it's used mainly in scientific research and electricity production.

Do rocks float on water? Pumice does. Pumice is formed when lava comes into contact with water. The rapid cooling of the hot lava creates bubbles as it turns the lava into solid rock. The bubbles in the rock make it less dense and allow the dry rock to float on water.

Get out of my way!

Want to make a pearl necklace disappear? Pour vinegar on it! Vinegar is an acid. Pearls are made of calcium carbonate. When these two substances mix, a chemical reaction occurs. The reaction dissolves the pearl and releases carbon dioxide. Small pearls measuring 0.33 inch (8.4 mm) can dissolve in just 72 hours.

What do you get when a metal that explodes in water and a yellow-green poisonous gas chemically react with one another? Something you use every day—ordinary table salt. The chemical name for table salt is sodium chloride. In its pure form, sodium is a metal that reacts violently with water. Chlorine is a poisonous gas. But when they chemically react with one another, they make harmless table salt.

The periodic table of elements includes the 118 known chemical elements. Each element has a one- or two-letter abbreviation, but two letters aren't found. What are they? J and Q.

FANTASTIC PHYSICS

What do floating frogs, cow manure, and air pressure all have in common? They're all involved in some fantastic physics facts.

If you have a powerful magnet, you can make a frog float on air! Like everything else in the world, frogs are made up of atoms. Atoms are made up of smaller units called electrons, protons, and neutrons. When an atom is put into a very strong magnetic field, the electrons in the atom shift their position slightly. This shift gives the atoms their own magnetic fields. The magnetic field of the frog's atoms and the external magnetic field repel each other. This causes the frog to levitate.

Let's float!

Water can't cut through steel, can it? It can if the water pressure is great enough. Water jets with pressures between 20,000 and 55,000 pounds per square inch (138 million and 379 million pascals) easily cut through steel up to 2 inches (5 cm) thick. A fine dusting of the gem garnet is added to the water jet to help it cut through the metal.

Microwave Magic

Something you probably use every day in your kitchen got its start spying for the military! In World War II (1939–1945), British scientists invented magnetron tubes, which produce microwaves. The tubes were installed in radar detectors to spot German airplanes. But that's not the end of the microwave's story. In 1946 scientist Percy Spencer was testing the magnetron tube when he realized that the tube's waves had melted a candy bar in his pocket. He then tested the microwaves to see if they would pop popcorn. They did—and the microwave oven was born. These early ovens were about the size of a refrigerator and sold for $5,000!

Farmers in Vermont are turning cow manure into power. The Audet family of rural Bridport, Vermont, owns more than 1,000 cows. Those cows produce a lot of manure. The Audets collect the poop in a big tank called a digester. There, bacteria break down the manure, producing methane gas. This gas is used as a fuel to make electricity. The Audets' cows produce enough poop to power about 400 homes!

Air doesn't weigh anything, does it? Wrong! Air pressure is created by compressed air molecules. About 1 ton (0.9 metric ton) of air pressure is on you at all times. That's about the weight of a small car!

Baseball fans know that a curveball is often harder to hit than a straight pitch. The curveball's spinning motion is the secret of its success. The spinning motion makes air flow differently over the top of the ball than it does under the ball. The air under the ball flows faster than the air on top of the ball. This forces the ball to move down or curve. This imbalance of force is called the Magnus Effect.

A substance can't be both a solid and a liquid at the same time, can it? It can if it's a mixture of cornstarch and water. Some people call the mixture oobleck. Oobleck acts like a solid when pressure is applied on it. Once the pressure is released, it flows like a liquid.

BIZARRE BIOLOGY

Did you know that you're not alone in your body? Or that a sneeze can spray snot as fast as a speeding car can travel? Plants, animals, and humans are sources of amazing facts.

Eww, nasty!

Not all flowers smell sweet. The titan arum, or corpse flower, actually smells like rotting flesh! The plant's stalk can reach 10 feet (3 m) tall. The flowers are 3 to 4 feet (0.9 to 1.2 m) wide. The plant can live many years without producing a flower. But once the flower blooms, plug your nose! People can smell its horrible odor 0.5 mile (0.8 km) away.

Like fingerprints, everyone's tongue print is unique.

It's hard to believe, but most of the cells in your body don't even belong to you. The bacteria living in your body outnumbers your cells by 10 to 1! Some of the bacteria are helpful, but others can cause disease.

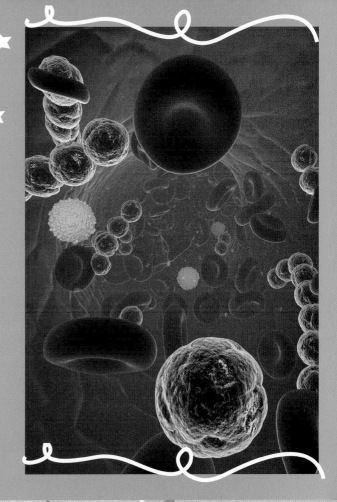

liver ⭐

The liver is the only human organ that can regenerate itself. A person can give part of his or her liver to another person, and the liver will grow back!

There's a good reason to cover your mouth when you sneeze. A sneeze can blast out of your nose and mouth at 100 miles (161 km) per hour! The spray can spread out 5 feet (1.5 m).

Do your feet stink when you take off your shoes? Your feet have more sweat glands than any other part of your body. Between the two of them, they have about 500,000 sweat glands. But that's not why feet stink. Sweat is basically water and salt. It doesn't smell at all. But bacteria love to munch on salty sweat, and they produce waste. This waste creates a smell that will clear a room when you kick off your shoes!

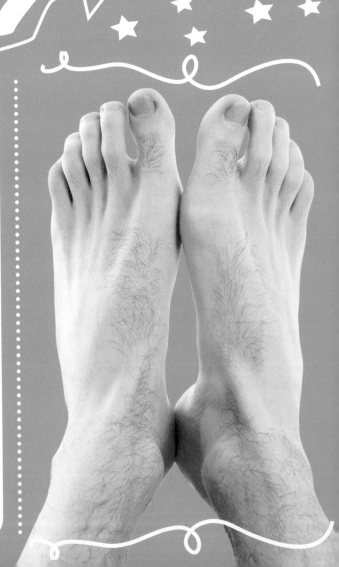

Have you ever had glowing red eyes on a photo? Don't worry—you're not turning into a werewolf. The pupil of your eye is just an opening that lets light into the eye. The flash of a camera can send light into the pupil and light up the retina on the inside of the eye. Retinas are mostly red. So the red-eye in the photo is actually a picture of the inside of your eye!

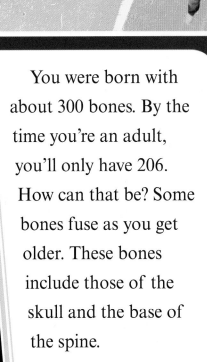

You were born with about 300 bones. By the time you're an adult, you'll only have 206. How can that be? Some bones fuse as you get older. These bones include those of the skull and the base of the spine.

The bark of a giant sequoia tree wouldn't make good firewood—it's fire-resistant! The spongy bark on these mature redwoods can be more than 2 feet (0.6 m) thick. The bark's thickness and the amount of water it contains help protect the trees from forest fires.

Can something that's been frozen for millions of years come back to life? Scientists have successfully revived 8-million-year-old bacteria found under ice in Antarctica. Once thawed, the bacteria went back to doing what bacteria do—reproducing.

Ever tried to have a stare-down with a baby? Infants blink only once or twice a minute. Adults blink an average of 10 times per minute. Babies' eyelid openings are smaller in relation to the eye. So a baby's eyes may not become dry as quickly as an adult's.

Stare me down! I dare you!

Why do your fingers and toes wrinkle after a long soak in the bathtub or swimming pool? You have extra amounts of dead skin on your fingers and toes. This dead skin absorbs water. It then wrinkles as it expands in size.

OUT OF THIS WORLD

These out-of-this-world facts come from outside Earth's atmosphere. Learn about Earth's growing weight problem and how to make Saturn float.

If you had a swimming pool that was 75,000 miles (120,700 km) wide, you could float Saturn in it! Saturn is made up mainly of hydrogen and helium. It is the least dense of all the planets. With a density less than that of water, Saturn could float.

Astronauts can be up to 2 inches (5 cm) taller in space. There is less gravity in space than there is on Earth. This allows the bones in the astronauts' backbones to stretch out, making them taller. Once they return to Earth's gravity, they return to their normal height.

Does Earth need to go on a diet? Earth gains weight every day from meteorites and other debris falling from space. Scientists estimate that Earth gains 37,000 to 78,000 tons (33,565 to 70,760 metric tons) per year.

Your weight doesn't change if you travel, right? Not so fast! If you weigh 100 pounds (45 kg) on Earth, you would weigh only 17 pounds (8 kg) on the moon. On Jupiter, you'd weigh 236 pounds (107 kg). No matter where you go in the universe, you have the same amount of mass. But your weight depends on gravity. On planets that have less gravity than Earth, you weigh less. On planets with more gravity, you weigh more.

Venus ★

The closer you are to the Sun, the hotter you are, right? Not always! Even though Mercury is the closest planet to the Sun, Venus is the hottest planet in our solar system. Venus' dense atmosphere contains both sulfuric acid and carbon dioxide, which help trap the Sun's heat. The temperature on Venus is about 870°F (465°C).

Is there sound in space? Actually, no. Sound waves need to travel through a medium, such as air or water. Space is a vacuum containing no molecules, so the sound waves don't travel.

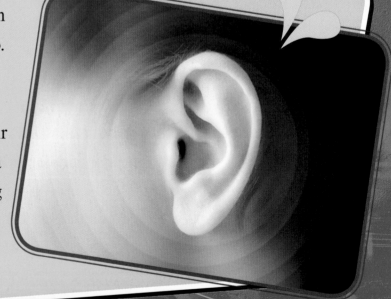

SEEING IS BELIEVING

The bizarre world of science reaches far beyond your school's laboratory. Why stop now? Keep your eyes and ears open for more wild and wonderful facts about the world of science!

CHAPTER FOUR

COOL

U.S. HISTORY

TRIVIA

AMERICA'S LOST HISTORY

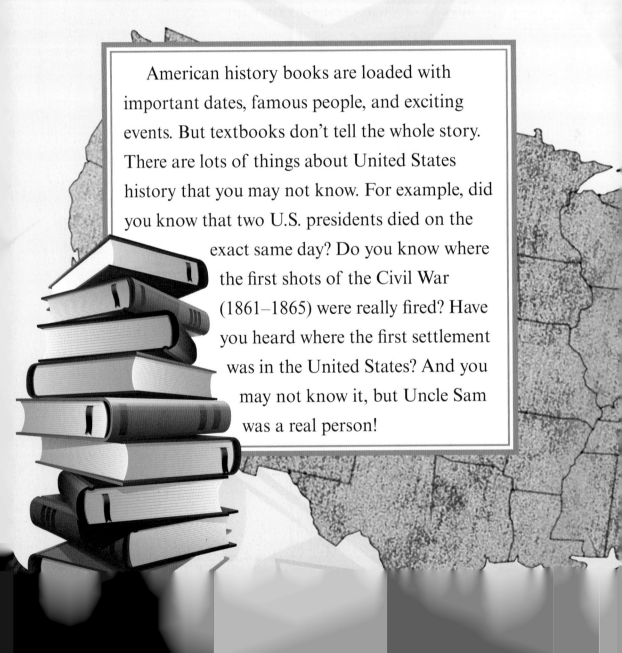

American history books are loaded with important dates, famous people, and exciting events. But textbooks don't tell the whole story. There are lots of things about United States history that you may not know. For example, did you know that two U.S. presidents died on the exact same day? Do you know where the first shots of the Civil War (1861–1865) were really fired? Have you heard where the first settlement was in the United States? And you may not know it, but Uncle Sam was a real person!

Get ready to revise what you think you know. This chapter is filled with little-known facts about the states, people, and events that helped shape U.S. history. Soon you will be able to impress your friends with your newfound knowledge about America's history.

UNUSUAL LOCATION FACTS

Many locations across the United States have mysterious pasts. The history of these places has been overlooked or simply forgotten. Find out the truth about America's first colony and several other U.S. locations.

In 1784 several counties in western North Carolina decided to become the state of Franklin, named for Benjamin Franklin. However, the rest of North Carolina's citizens didn't like the idea. They encouraged Congress to vote against the move. When it was time to vote, Congress said "no" to Franklin.

Plymouth, Massachusetts, was not the original destination of the Pilgrims. They had hoped to settle along the Hudson River in New York. The land there was good for farming. But travel delays and the arrival of winter forced the Pilgrims to settle in Plymouth instead.

California is known for its oranges. However, oranges are not native to California. The first two orange trees were brought to California from Brazil in 1873. They were planted in Riverside, California. Most of the oldest California orange trees come from those two trees.

St. Augustine, Florida

Jamestown, Virginia, was not the first colony in the United States. The first permanent European colony was actually St. Augustine, Florida. This Spanish colony was formed in 1565—42 years before Jamestown.

The United States has had three capitals since the U.S. Constitution was written in 1787. New York City served as the capital from 1789 to 1790. Then Philadelphia became the capital until 1800. Finally, in November of that year Washington, D.C., opened as the capital city.

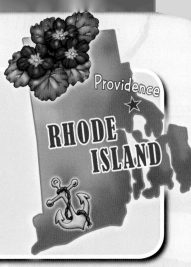

Rhode Island is the smallest state in total area. But it has the longest official name of any U.S. state. Its official name is "The State of Rhode Island and Providence Plantations."

In Europe during the 1700s, a lot of people had trouble paying their bills. These people were often arrested and put into debtor's prisons. But these prisons soon became overcrowded. In 1733 James Oglethorpe decided to solve the problem by creating the colony of Georgia in North America. Debtors were sent to Georgia to help reduce prison populations. Working in the new colony also gave debtors a chance to pay off their bills.

CONFOUNDING COINCIDENCES

Sometimes events have strange connections to other events. These strange coincidences often happen when we least expect them. The following coincidences from U.S. history will make you stop and say, "No way!"

McLean home at Appomattox Court House, Virginia

In 1861 Wilmer McLean's home was located near Manassas, Virginia. The first major battle of the Civil War was the Battle of Bull Run, which took place on McLean's property. McLean later moved to the town of Appomattox Court House, Virginia. But he could not escape the war. In 1865 the Confederate Army surrendered to the Union—at McLean's house! After this event McLean supposedly said, "The war began in my front yard and ended in my front parlor."

John Adams and Thomas Jefferson had a lot in common. They both helped write the Declaration of Independence. They both served as U.S. president. And they both died on Independence Day in 1826—exactly 50 years after the Declaration of Independence was signed.

Robert E. Lee was the leader of the Confederate Army in the Civil War. But did you know President Abraham Lincoln once asked him to lead the Union Army? Lee opposed slavery and didn't think Southern states should secede from the Union. However, he was loyal to his home state of Virginia. He turned down Lincoln's offer, and chose to command Virginia's forces instead. Lee later became the general-in-chief of the Confederate Army.

William McKinley

The 23rd regiment from Ohio fought bravely in the Civil War. Two future U.S. presidents served in the 23rd. One of the generals was Rutherford B. Hayes, who later became the 19th U.S. president. As an officer, Hayes twice promoted a soldier he considered courageous in battle. This soldier was William McKinley, who would go on to become America's 25th president.

Rutherford B. Hayes

The first lifelong slave in America was actually owned by a former indentured servant. In the 1600s these servants worked for a time in the American colonies and then were freed. Anthony Johnson was one such servant. He came from Africa, earned his freedom, and later owned a farm and servants of his own. In 1640 he caught his servant John Casor trying to run away. He took Casor to court, which later ruled that Casor was Johnson's "servant for life."

Samuel Adams was one of the most important leaders of the Revolutionary War (1775–1783). He led the Boston Sons of Liberty in their fight for freedom. And he often made speeches to protest British taxation. But his earlier job might surprise you. From 1756 to 1764 he worked as a British tax collector in Massachusetts.

Robert Todd Lincoln

You may know that John Wilkes Booth assassinated Abraham Lincoln. But did you know that Booth's brother Edwin once saved a Lincoln? One day in 1864, Edwin was waiting at a train station in Jersey City, New Jersey. When he saw a young man fall into the space between a train and the platform, he rushed into action. Edwin grabbed the young man by the collar and pulled him up, just as the train began to move. The man Edwin rescued was none other than Robert Todd Lincoln—Abraham's son!

AMAZING EVENTS

The Revolutionary War, the Lewis and Clark expedition, and the Civil War all changed the course of U.S. history. However, these events and others included episodes that might surprise you.

Most Americans believe the United States declared its independence from Great Britain on July 4, 1776. But that isn't quite true. The Continental Congress actually voted to declare independence on July 2. But Congress did not officially approve the final text of the Declaration of Independence until July 4.

James Madison's wife, Dolley, saved a big part of U.S. history during the War of 1812 (1812–1815). In 1814 the British attempted to burn down the White House. Before she fled the burning building, Dolley saved several important papers. These documents included the Declaration of Independence and the first draft of the U.S. Constitution.

In 1587 Governor John White left the English colony on Roanoke Island in North Carolina to bring back supplies from England. But a war between England and Spain prevented him from returning until 1590. When he returned, the people of Roanoke had disappeared. The mystery was never solved. Roanoke eventually became known as "The Lost Colony." Historians believe that American Indians or nearby Spanish settlers may have attacked the colony. Others think the colonists simply joined one of the local American Indian tribes.

Robert L. Livingston is often a forgotten patriot. He helped write the Declaration of Independence, but he never put his name on it. He had to return to his job in New York before he could sign it.

One of the most important battles in the Revolutionary War was the Battle of Bunker Hill in 1775. However, the battle did not actually take place on Bunker Hill. The colonists had planned to take control of Bunker Hill. But as they made their move during the night, they accidentally took over nearby Breed's Hill instead. Some historians believe that a map error led to the Americans taking the wrong hill.

Sacagawea is famous for helping Meriwether Lewis and William Clark on their expedition to the West. But no one really knows if Sacagawea was her real name. Sacagawea was a Shoshone Indian. As a child she had been kidnapped and forced to live with the Hidatsa tribe. She may have taken a new name with the Hidatsa.

The 1849 Gold Rush in California was not the first time gold was discovered in the United States. When gold was discovered in Dahlonega, Georgia, it sparked a gold rush about 21 years earlier.

Georgia

MONUMENTAL MARVELS

Major monuments like Mount Rushmore and the Statue of Liberty symbolize American freedoms. However, there is more to these symbols than meets the eye. Secrets and mysteries surround several U.S. monuments that few people have ever heard about.

The famous Liberty Bell in Philadelphia, Pennsylvania, has an outdated spelling. Pennsylvania is actually spelled *Pensylvania* on the bell. In 1753 there was no official way to spell Pennsylvania. The Liberty Bell spelling was acceptable at the time. The U.S. Constitution contains the same outdated spelling.

The Statue of Liberty has gone through a lot of changes since it was first dedicated in 1886. First, its official name, "Liberty Enlightening the World," has almost been forgotten. The statue's original torch was replaced in 1986. And the color of the statue has changed over time. The statue is made of copper and originally had a shiny red-brown color. A chemical change called patination has given the copper statue its current greenish color.

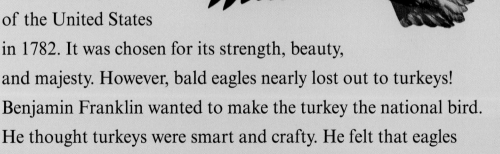

The bald eagle became the symbol of the United States in 1782. It was chosen for its strength, beauty, and majesty. However, bald eagles nearly lost out to turkeys! Benjamin Franklin wanted to make the turkey the national bird. He thought turkeys were smart and crafty. He felt that eagles were cowardly and unfit to symbolize America.

"Plymouth Rock" In Front of Pilgrim Hall "1834"
Copyright A.W. Anderson
1620

Some history books say that the Pilgrims landed at Plymouth Rock in Massachusetts. But the Pilgrims never mention the rock in their writings. In 1741 a man named Elder Faunce declared the rock to be the Pilgrim stepping-stone. Faunce claimed that his father knew several Pilgrims who had told him about the rock. Faunce's story was told and retold for many years. In 1774 the residents of Plymouth placed the rock in front of the town's meetinghouse. An iron fence was later built around the rock to help keep it safe. The story of Plymouth Rock has been part of the Pilgrim story ever since.

The Gateway Arch in St. Louis, Missouri, symbolizes the city's status as the "Gateway to the West." During the 1800s St. Louis was the last stop before many settlers headed west. The city also served as a base camp for the famous Lewis and Clark expedition. At 630 feet (192 m) tall, the Gateway Arch is the tallest man-made monument in the United States. It is taller than both the Washington Monument and the Statue of Liberty.

Mount Rushmore was originally designed to have a secret vault behind the presidential heads. Designer Gutzon Borglum wanted the vault to be a Hall of Records for copies of important U.S. documents. Borglum died before the hall could be completed. However his dream lived on. In 1998 the U.S. government finished the hall. Copies of the Declaration of Independence, the U.S. Constitution, and the Bill of Rights were sealed inside a vault that is meant to last for thousands of years.

PECULIAR
PRESIDENTS

U.S. presidents hold many important roles like chief executive and commander in chief of the armed forces. However, like all people, presidents' lives often include unusual events.

U.S. President James Madison took his role of commander in chief of the military seriously. During the War of 1812, Madison tried to take command on the battlefield when the British army invaded Washington, D.C. However, he proved ineffective and had to retreat with the soldiers. Madison became the first and only U.S. president to face enemy fire in battle while holding the office.

William Henry Harrison served the shortest time of any U.S. president. The country's ninth president served for just 31 days. On March 4, 1841, he became sick on his first day as president. His cold later turned to pneumonia, which caused his death.

President Harry S. Truman had no middle name. His parents could not decide which of his grandfathers, Solomon Young or Anderson Shippe, to use for his middle name. Rather than picking one name, Harry's parents settled on a simple "S" instead.

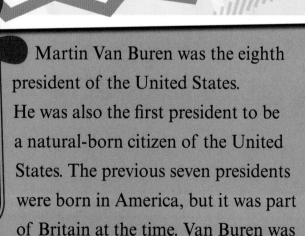

Martin Van Buren was the eighth president of the United States. He was also the first president to be a natural-born citizen of the United States. The previous seven presidents were born in America, but it was part of Britain at the time. Van Buren was born December 5, 1782—more than six years after the Declaration of Independence was signed.

Gerald Ford

Talk about luck. Gerald Ford was the only person to serve as both vice president and president and never be voted into either office. In 1973 Ford was serving as the Speaker of the House in the U.S. House of Representatives. When Vice President Spiro Agnew was forced to resign, Ford was chosen to replace him. Then Ford became president when Richard Nixon resigned in 1974.

Abraham Lincoln (left)

As a young man, President Abraham Lincoln had an interesting pastime—he was a wrestler! In 1831 Lincoln was living in New Salem, Illinois. A group of rowdy men known as the Clary's Grove Boys liked to challenge people to wrestling matches. One day a local grocer said that his clerk could beat their best wrestler. The groups' leader, Jack Armstrong, took up the challenge. "Honest Abe" soundly defeated Armstrong in one of several matches he fought in town.

John Tyler is the only U.S. president to eventually turn against his own country. In 1841 John Tyler was elected as vice president. When President William Henry Harrison died, Tyler became president until 1845. But when the Civil War broke out, Tyler joined the Confederacy.

John Tyler

The longest serving president was Franklin D. Roosevelt. He was elected to the office four times. He led the United States during the Great Depression in the 1930s and at the beginning of World War II (1939–1945). Roosevelt died on April 12, 1945, shortly after starting his fourth term. He served 4,422 days in office. Later a constitutional amendment limited presidents to serving two four-year terms in office.

INCREDIBLE
INCIDENTS

U.S. history is filled with many famous stories. However, sometimes the stories didn't happen quite the way you might remember. Take a look at the truth behind some of these historical events.

Most history books say the Civil War started with the battle at Fort Sumter in South Carolina on April 12, 1861. But the first shots were actually fired three months earlier. On January 9, 1861, southern soldiers on Morris Island, South Carolina, opened fire on the Union steamship *Star of the West*. The ship was taking supplies to Fort Sumter.

Paul Revere was not the only person who made the famous midnight ride on April 18, 1775. William Dawes and Samuel Prescott also rode out to warn people that British soldiers were coming. Why do we remember Revere and not the others? Revere was made famous by a poem written by Henry Wadsworth Longfellow.

The first Thanksgiving may not have been celebrated by the Pilgrims. On September 8, 1565, explorer Pedro Menedez de Aviles celebrated a thanksgiving feast in what is now St. Augustine, Florida. He dined with the local Timucua Indians. And turkey wasn't the main food for the day. They ate bean soup instead!

John Hanson

If you thought the first U.S. president was George Washington, you'd be wrong. George Washington did serve as the first president elected under the U.S. Constitution. However, from 1777 to 1789, the country had an earlier constitution called the Articles of Confederation. The Continental Congress was responsible at this time for electing presidents to lead the country. The first president to serve under the full Articles of Confederation was John Hanson.

According to legend, no Americans survived the Battle of the Alamo in 1836. But some historians think a few defenders of the Alamo may have survived the fight, including Davy Crockett. However, after the battle the Mexican army supposedly executed them.

Uncle Sam isn't just a cartoon character seen in posters. He was actually a real person. Samuel Wilson had a meat-packing business in New York. In the 1800s he supplied meat to soldiers in the army. His company put the initials "U.S." on its packages. During the War of 1812, soldiers began referring to "U.S." as "Uncle Sam" Wilson. Soon Uncle Sam became as American as apple pie. The cartoon image we know today as Uncle Sam was first drawn by Thomas Nast in 1869.

HUNTING FOR HISTORY TRIVIA

As you can see, a lot of little-known facts about U.S. history are just waiting to be found. Keep researching the important people and events that have shaped U.S. history. You may find something interesting that will surprise your family and friends!

CHAPTER FIVE

AWESOME SPORTS TRIVIA

INCREDIBLE SPORTS

Can you imagine the world without sports? It's not a pretty thought. A world with no skateboards, no Super Bowl, and no Olympics would be a sad place.

Sports have been around almost as long as people have lived on Earth. Ancient people threw, kicked, and caught balls. They wrestled each other. They raced. And they developed rules about how their sports should be played. Sports give us plenty of reasons to play. This chapter is a collection of everything that's fun about the world of sports!

AMAZING ATHLETES

The greatest athletes never stop pushing the limits. That winning spirit was clear in the tiny gymnast who showed the world perfection. It was there in the baseball player who took the field for every game during 16 seasons. These athletes and others have expanded the limits of what's possible.

During his 27-year career, Major League Baseball (MLB) pitcher Nolan Ryan made failure a family affair when he struck out eight fathers and their sons. They were Bobby and Barry Bonds; Ken and Ken Griffey Jr.; Maury and Bump Wills; Sandy, Sandy Jr., and Roberto Alomar; Hal and Brian McRae; Dick and Dick Jr. Schofield; Tony and Eduardo Perez; and Tito and Terry Francona.

Former National Basketball Association (NBA) player Shaquille O'Neal's shoe size is 22. The average shoe size for men is 10.5!

Sports fans were amazed when Bo Jackson and Deion Sanders played both pro baseball and football. For Jim Thorpe, two sports was a slow year! In the 1912 Olympics, Thorpe won gold medals in the decathlon and the pentathlon. Thorpe was a pro football star from 1913 until 1928. He also played six years of Major League Baseball and toured with a pro basketball team.

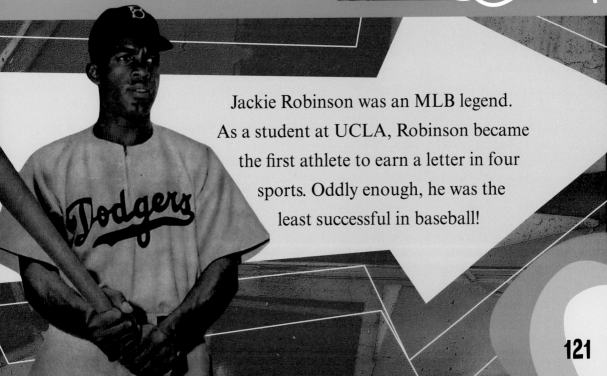

Jackie Robinson was an MLB legend. As a student at UCLA, Robinson became the first athlete to earn a letter in four sports. Oddly enough, he was the least successful in baseball!

You don't earn a nickname like "The Great One" without breaking a few records. Wayne Gretzky holds or shares 61 National Hockey League (NHL) records. His 2,857 career points are almost 1,000 points more than any other hockey player. Gretzky is the only NHL player to total more than 200 points in a single season. And he did it four times!

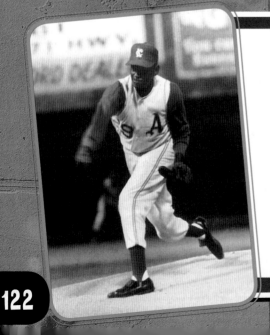

The great Satchel Paige is the oldest player to appear in an MLB game. In 1965, 59-year-old Paige pitched for the Kansas City A's. He shut down the Boston Red Sox for three innings.

Even great athletes have to practice. Tony Hawk spent 10 years trying to nail skateboarding's most difficult trick, the 900. At the 1999 X Games, Hawk dropped off the half-pipe and spun around 2½ times in the air. He had landed the first 900!

Wilt "The Stilt" Chamberlain was an NBA record-setting machine. Chamberlain, who played from 1959 to 1974, still holds 72 NBA records. His most famous record is his 100-point game against the New York Knicks in 1962. During his career, Chamberlain never fouled out of a game. And during the 1961–62 NBA season, Chamberlain played almost every minute of every game. Except for a six-minute stretch in one game, he stayed on the court from the tip-off to the final buzzer.

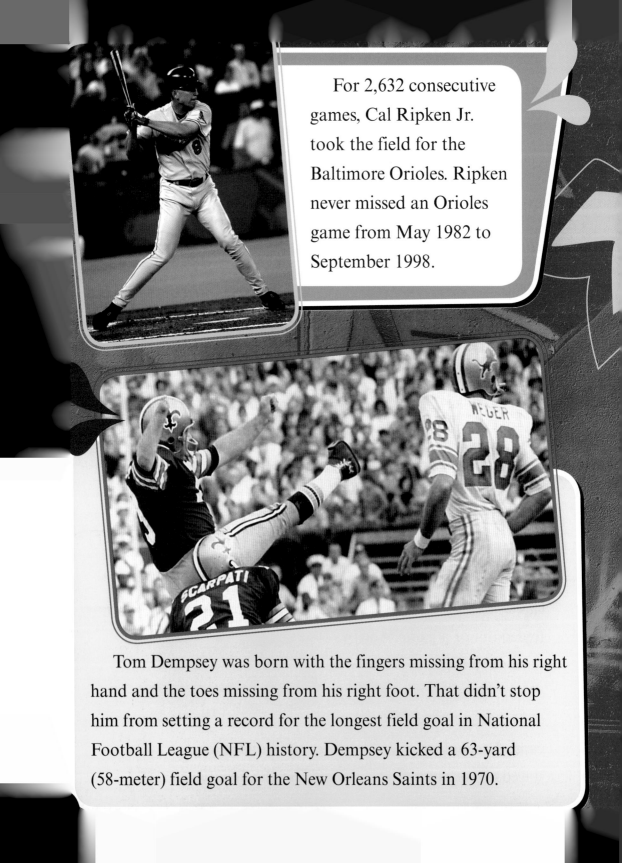

For 2,632 consecutive games, Cal Ripken Jr. took the field for the Baltimore Orioles. Ripken never missed an Orioles game from May 1982 to September 1998.

Tom Dempsey was born with the fingers missing from his right hand and the toes missing from his right foot. That didn't stop him from setting a record for the longest field goal in National Football League (NFL) history. Dempsey kicked a 63-yard (58-meter) field goal for the New Orleans Saints in 1970.

Reggie Jackson, Albert Pujols, and Babe Ruth are the only players to hit three home runs in a single World Series game. In Game 6 of the 1977 World Series, Jackson hit his three home runs on the first pitch of his last three at bats—three pitches, three swings, and three home runs.

Babe Ruth ★

Cy Young must have had a tired right arm. Young owns the MLB record for career pitching wins (511), losses (316), and innings pitched (7,356). MLB honored him by naming the award for the season's best pitcher the Cy Young Award.

Fourteen-year-old Nadia Comaneci charmed the entire world at the 1976 Montreal Olympics. The girl from Romania became the first gymnast to score a perfect 10. She finished with seven perfect 10s and three gold medals!

Who says football is only for guys? In 1997 kicker Liz Heaston became the first female player to score in a college football game. Heaston kicked two extra points to help win a game for Oregon's Willamette University.

On September 23, 1992, Manon Rheaume became the first woman to play in one of the four major U.S. pro sports leagues. She played goalie for the Tampa Bay Lightning in a pre-season game.

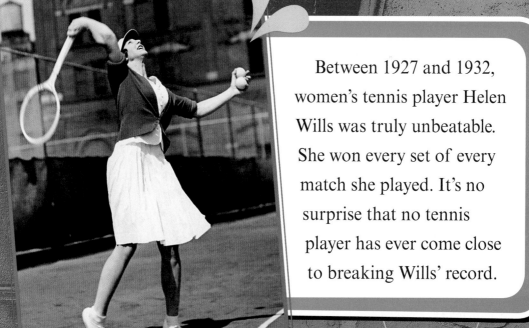

Between 1927 and 1932, women's tennis player Helen Wills was truly unbeatable. She won every set of every match she played. It's no surprise that no tennis player has ever come close to breaking Wills' record.

TREMENDOUS TEAMS

When teams work together and play well, they inspire their fans. With thousands of fans behind them, teams can achieve more than they could by themselves.

The 1972 Miami Dolphins are the only NFL team to finish an entire season with a perfect record. Since then, no NFL team has survived a season without at least one loss.

There is only one U.S. city where each major sports team wears the same colors. The Pittsburgh Penguins, Steelers, and Pirates all wear black and gold.

In 2008 the University of Connecticut women's basketball team started an amazing winning streak. When the Lady Huskies finally lost in 2010, they had won 90 straight games and two National Collegiate Athletic Association (NCAA) titles.

The 1916 Georgia Tech football team scored more points in one game than any two teams combined. The Yellow Jackets crushed Cumberland College of Tennessee, 222-0. This score still stands as a record for most points by one football team and most points scored in one football game.

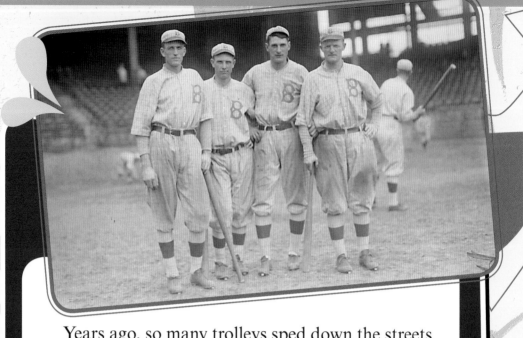

Years ago, so many trolleys sped down the streets of Brooklyn, New York, that people there were called "trolley-dodgers." When it came time to name their baseball team, the Dodgers made perfect sense. Now that the team is in Los Angeles, the meaning is lost.

Only nine major sports teams in the United States and Canada have a nickname that doesn't end with an "s."

What's with the name?

Have you ever wondered why the Los Angeles NBA team is called the Lakers? Los Angeles sits beside the Pacific Ocean, but there aren't many lakes there. The Lakers moved to Los Angeles from Minneapolis, known as the City of Lakes.

NFL helmets were just plain boring until 1948. That year, the Los Angeles Rams painted yellow horns on their helmets. Today the Cleveland Browns are the only team without a helmet logo.

UNEXPECTED EVENTS

Sports events don't have a script. There is always a chance that something unexpected could happen.

Today a Super Bowl ticket can cost more than $1,000. But the tickets weren't always so valued. At Super Bowl I in 1967, the Los Angeles Memorial Coliseum had more than 30,000 empty seats. Some tickets sold for as little as $6!

In a 1993 AFC playoff game, the Buffalo Bills trailed the Houston Oilers 35-3 in the second half. Many Bills fans figured their team had no chance to win and left. These fans were sorry later when the Bills scored four touchdowns to win 41-38 in overtime.

On December 31, 1967, the Green Bay Packers and Dallas Cowboys faced off in the legendary Ice Bowl. It was the NFL title game. The winner wasn't decided until the last second. But it was the cold that made the game memorable. The temperature in Green Bay, Wisconsin, at game time was -13°F (-25°C). Nearly two dozen fans went to the hospital suffering from exposure, and four had heart attacks. Tragically, one died.

Unusual Adventures

Each member of the NHL championship team gets to spend a day with the event trophy, the Stanley Cup. Over the years, the cup has been part of some unusual adventures. Martin Brodeur of the 2003 New Jersey Devils ate popcorn out of it at a movie theater. In 1906 the Montreal Wanderers took the cup to a photographer's house for a team photo. The team left the house without the cup. The photographer's mother found it and planted flowers in it. In 1980 the New York Islanders' Clark Gillies let his dog eat out of the cup. Since 1995 the cup has had a 24-hour bodyguard. Players can still have fun with the cup, but the bodyguard is always there to protect it.

OUTRAGEOUS
AWESOME SPORTS
TRIVIA

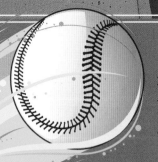

There are only two days during the year in which there is no MLB, NBA, NHL, or NFL game. They occur the day before and the day after the MLB All-Star game.

Stretching is good!

The seventh-inning stretch is part of all MLB games. It's believed to have started at Manhattan College in 1882. During a game, baseball coach Brother Jasper Brennan saw that the crowd was restless. In the seventh inning, he turned and urged the fans to stand up and stretch. The stretch caught on and soon spread to the major leagues.

Only one pitcher has thrown a perfect game in the World Series. New York Yankee Don Larsen pitched a perfect game in Game 5 of the 1956 World Series.

Since the World Series began in 1903, it has been held during two world wars and an earthquake. But there were two years it didn't happen. In 1904 the New York Giants of the National League refused to play the American League champs, the Boston Americans. In 1994 MLB players went on strike, and the World Series had to be canceled.

Where are all the fans?

During a NASCAR race, the temperature inside the cars climbs as high as 140°F (60°C). Drivers can lose 5 to 10 pounds (2.3 to 4.5 kg) during a race.

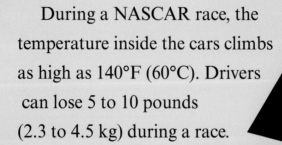

At 200 miles (322 km) per hour, a NASCAR car can travel 293 feet (89 m) in one second. That's nearly the length of a football field!

During turns NASCAR drivers can experience 3 units of g-force against their bodies. This is the same amount of force that astronauts on a space shuttle experience at liftoff!

Wimbledon is the world's most famous tennis tournament. In 2010 it was the site of the longest professional tennis match—11 hours and 5 minutes. John Isner and Nicolas Mahut began playing the evening of June 22 before darkness fell. The match resumed June 23 before again being called for darkness. After an hour of play on June 24, Isner finally won.

Is a race still a race with only one competitor? Triple Crown winner Citation entered the 1948 Pimlico Special along with 20 other racehorses. When the other owners saw Citation was running, they got scared and pulled their horses out of the race. Citation ran the race alone.

STRANGE BUT TRUE

Sports are always a little bit out of the ordinary. From a sport founded by a toy maker to boxers knocking each other out at the same time, sports supply a lot of strange surprises.

In 2005 skateboarder Danny Way decided to jump over the Great Wall of China. The wall is 61 feet (19 m) wide. Way designed a ramp to help him jump over the wall. He cleared the wall five times, even doing tricks during some of the jumps.

Piece of cake!

Most kids use a baseball until it falls apart. But a baseball used in MLB games has an average life span of only six pitches. With between 250 and 300 pitches per game, that's 49 to 50 balls that don't make it to the next game!

Freestyle motocross star Travis Pastrana had an extreme dream. In 2001 he made it come true. He used a parachute to jump his motorcycle into the Grand Canyon. He free-fell 1,000 feet (305 m) and then pulled the parachute, which allowed him to float the last 500 feet (152 m) to the canyon floor.

Can you believe a major sport started with a toy? In 1965 Sherman Popper invented a toy called a Snurfer, which was short for "snow surfer." It was basically two skis tied together, with a rope at the front for steering. Popper's invention led to the snowboards of today.

Shortstop Zoilo Versalles threw away his baseball glove after every error. During Versalles' 12-year MLB career, he made 284 errors. That's a lot of baseball gloves! But pitcher Jim Kaat found a glove he really liked—he used the same one for 15 seasons!

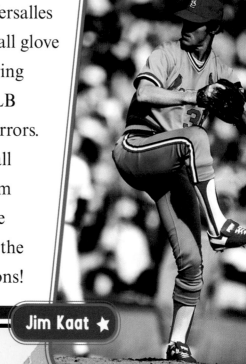

Jim Kaat ★

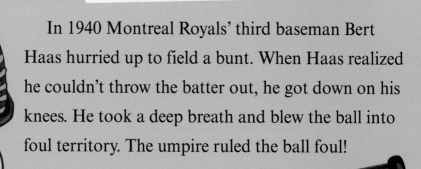

In 1940 Montreal Royals' third baseman Bert Haas hurried up to field a bunt. When Haas realized he couldn't throw the batter out, he got down on his knees. He took a deep breath and blew the ball into foul territory. The umpire ruled the ball foul!

The sport of stock car racing traces its roots to bootleggers of the 1920s. To get away from the police, bootleggers modified their cars to handle high speeds and sharp turns. Soon the bootleggers began racing each other. The races started to attract crowds, and stock car racing was born.

If you want your team to win the Super Bowl, make sure your quarterback wears number 12! A quarterback wearing that number has played for the winning team in 1969, 1972–80, 2002, 2004–05, and 2011.

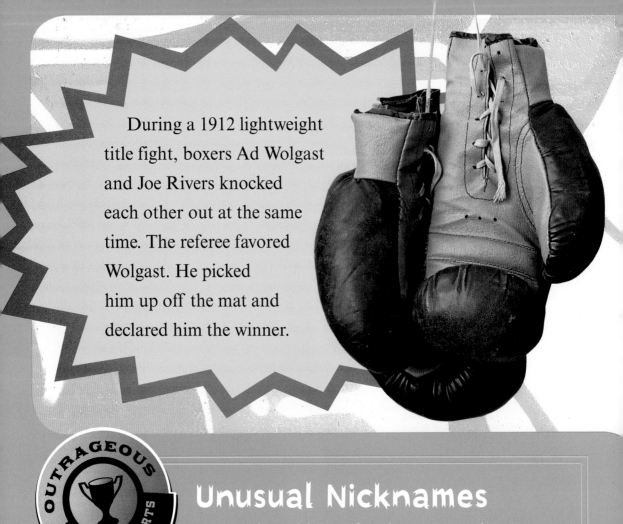

During a 1912 lightweight title fight, boxers Ad Wolgast and Joe Rivers knocked each other out at the same time. The referee favored Wolgast. He picked him up off the mat and declared him the winner.

Unusual Nicknames

Popular athletes often have unusual nicknames. Chicago Bears nosetackle William "The Refrigerator" Perry measured 6 feet, 2 inches (188 cm) and weighed 325 pounds (147 kg) in his playing days. Fans thought he looked like a refrigerator. Race car driver A.J. "Fancy Pants" Foyt earned his nickname by showing up for races in silk shirts and white pants. And Larry "Lawnmower" Csonka was a tough running back for the Miami Dolphins in the 1970s. He didn't pick up his feet when he ran, so teammates said he looked like a lawnmower.

WORLD OF SPORTS

The world of sports can be crazy, amazing, and just plain wacky, but most of all, it's fun. Whether you're an athlete or a fan, there's much to love about the wild, wonderful world of sports!

CHAPTER SIX

AMAZING WEATHER TRIVIA

ALL KINDS OF WEATHER

Have you ever seen watermelon snow or hissing, exploding ball lighting? Or a snowflake the size of a pizza? And did you know bees and sharks predict weather?

Weather is something we experience every day. But it's much more than wind, rain, snow, and sunshine. The world of weather is full of facts that are almost too amazing to be true. Have fun discovering the world's weirdest, wildest weather trivia!

STORM AHEAD

ZAP AND BOOM

Flash! Bolts of lightning slash across the sky. Rain drums on the roof. Thunder roars and booms. Wind rattles windows, and tree branches crash to the ground. Powerful thunderstorms can cause plenty of damage and strange events.

What was so odd about Shenandoah National Park Ranger Roy Sullivan? He was nicknamed the Human Lightning Rod. Between 1942 and 1977, he was zapped seven times—most likely by a bolt that hit something he was touching. Two of those times, his hair caught fire!

Just how hot is lightning? Lightning can heat the air in its path to 50,000°F (27,760°C). That's five times hotter than the sun's surface!

Central Florida is known as the lightning capital of the United States. During an average August in Brevard County, Florida, lightning strikes more than 6,000 times!

A statue in Lexington, Kentucky, has the worst luck around. A powerful thunderstorm in July 1903 hit a statue of politician Henry Clay that stood atop a 120-foot (37-m) stone column. The storm knocked off the statue's 350-pound (159-kg) head. The headless statue was fixed in May 1910. Four months later, lightning shattered the statue again. Now it has a lightning rod for protection.

Lightning is attracted to tall buildings. Lightning strikes the 1,454-foot (443-m) Empire State Building in New York City about 100 times each year.

Mysterious ball lightning slips inside houses through windows, doors, or chimneys. As large as a soccer ball or as tiny as a grape, some ball lightning glows bright white. Or it can be red, orange, yellow, green, blue, or violet. It bounces, floats, buzzes, and hisses. Then it disappears or explodes. Scientists still aren't sure what causes it.

Cows and lightning don't mix. To escape from a storm, cows often huddle under trees. If lightning hits the trees, it can kill the whole herd—31 in a single strike in Denmark in 2004. Or cows rush to a wire fence. Lightning zaps the fence and kills the cows—52 dead cows in Uruguay in October 2008.

It's a good rule to stay away from trees, metal fences, and cows during a thunderstorm!

No storm in sight. Bright, blue sky. Think lightning won't hit? Wrong! Lightning can strike 10 to 15 miles (16 to 24 km) away from a storm. These strikes are called bolts from the blue.

Hundreds of years ago, people in Europe thought noise scared away lightning storms. Men rushed to the top of towers to ring church bells. Not a good idea—nearly 400 bell towers were struck and more than 100 bell ringers died.

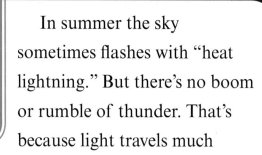

In summer the sky sometimes flashes with "heat lightning." But there's no boom or rumble of thunder. That's because light travels much faster than sound. You can see the lightning from a distant storm, but it's too far away to hear the thunder.

A woman struck and killed by lightning in Pennsylvania in 1994 was found with the zipper of her jeans melted. Plus, two coins in her pocket were fused together.

What could lightning and ribbons have in common? Ribbon lightning occurs when strong winds separate the strokes of the bolt, making it look like a wide ribbon.

At 120 decibels, thunder is almost as noisy as a jackhammer. Get too close, and you could have temporary deafness or even permanent hearing loss.

An average lightning bolt is 5 miles (8 km) long. The longest ever recorded spanned 118 miles (190 km) near Dallas, Texas!

During a thunderstorm, you can figure out the distance of lightning. When you see lightning, count the seconds until you hear thunder. Divide the number by five. The result is the number of miles between you and the lightning.

WHAT'S FALLING FROM THE SKY?

You never know what might fall from the sky. A heavy downpour could flatten your mom's flowers. Hail might pound dents in your family car. Snow may pile so high that schools and businesses close. Even frogs can fall from the sky!

Volleyball-sized hailstones pelted Vivian, South Dakota, on July 23, 2010. Imagine a 2-pound (0.9-kg) hailstone hitting your car or your house's roof. Clunk!

A deadly hailstorm in India on April 30, 1988, killed 246 people and about 1,600 animals. With no warning, the daytime sky turned black, and hailstones the size of baseballs pounded people before they could find shelter.

Snowflakes the size of large pizzas fell from the sky on January 28, 1887, at Fort Keough, Montana. The flakes were said to be 15 inches (38 cm) wide and 8 inches (20 cm) thick. When snow crystals clump together, gigantic snowflakes can form.

The bigger a hailstone, the faster it falls to the ground. Large hailstones can fall faster than 100 miles (161 km) per hour!

Keep your umbrella handy! Reports during the past hundreds of years describe frogs, fish, and even maggots tumbling from the sky. Researchers suspect tornadic waterspouts suck up the creatures and later drop them again.

Yellow snow? Might not be what you think—it could be algae. In very cold climates, algae can grow in snow, turning it yellow, blue, or brown. "Watermelon snow" in polar regions can be red or green and smells sweet, like a melon. Dust, sand, and pollen can also cause colored snow. You probably still shouldn't eat it.

The rain just wouldn't stop in Johnstown, Pennsylvania, late in May 1889. On May 31 the South Fork Dam on Lake Conemaugh gave way. Twenty million tons (18 million metric tons) of lake water roared down the valley. The flash flood and the fire that followed it killed 2,209 people, making it one of the worst disasters in U.S. history.

No one can control the weather, but people have tried. "Cloud seeding" began in the 1940s. Airplane pilots dropped dry ice pellets or silver iodide into clouds. These substances caused the clouds to develop snow, which melted into raindrops as it fell. People in some drought-stricken areas still use cloud seeding.

Lightning flashes and booming thunder during a snowstorm? It happens! Thundersnow can occur when a layer of moist, warm air near the ground pushes upward through a layer of cold air.

In Kerala, India, blood-red rain fell from the sky occasionally from late July to September 2001. Was it caused by red dust? Fungus spores? Or microbes from outer space? Nobody knows for sure.

STORMS CALLED TWISTERS

Also called twisters, tornadoes can be huge, incredibly powerful, and unpredictable. A tornado can demolish a house in a heartbeat or hop over and never touch it. A tornado can be skinny and funnel-shaped or so wide it's like a thick, dark wall of wind.

Keep your eyes on the sky if you live in Tornado Alley! In the center of the United States, tornadoes hit more often and are more severe. This is especially the case in Nebraska, Kansas, Oklahoma and Texas. But twisters can also strike almost anyplace else.

On April 3 and 4, 1974, a "Super Outbreak" caused 148 tornadoes in 13 states. In Xenia, Ohio, a school bus landed on a stage where high school students had been rehearsing a play! The students escaped just minutes before the tornado struck.

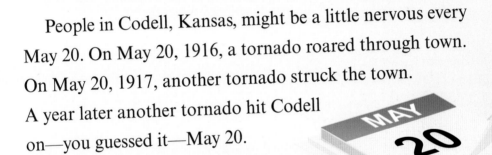

People in Codell, Kansas, might be a little nervous every May 20. On May 20, 1916, a tornado roared through town. On May 20, 1917, another tornado struck the town. A year later another tornado hit Codell on—you guessed it—May 20.

Tornado winds can do some very strange things. They can whisk away egg cartons without breaking eggs. Twisters can blow papers hundreds of miles away or jam a splinter into a metal fire hydrant. A tornado in Great Bend, Kansas, carried a tie rack 40 miles (64 km) away without losing the ties.

Ever seen spouts of water or dirt spinning in the air? Waterspouts can suck up fish and sink ships. Dust devils can be tiny whirlwinds of dirt or towers of spinning sand. Dust devils often last only a minute, but some contain tons of dust whirling thousands of feet high.

About 1,000 tornadoes rage through the United States each year, striking any month, any time, day or night. April 2011 had a record-breaking 758 tornadoes!

Can a tornado catch fire? No, but wildfires sometimes form a rotating column that looks much like a tornado. Fire whirls are usually caused by a great deal of heat produced in a small space. After the Great Kanto earthquake in Japan in 1923, a fire whirl killed 38,000 people trapped in downtown Tokyo.

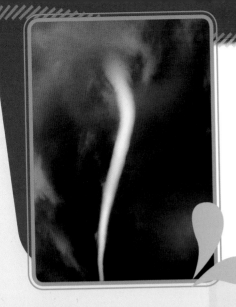

What color is a tornado? A tornado that forms in humid air may have a cloud inside it, making it appear white. Tornadoes can also be black, brown, red or gray, depending on the color of dirt and debris they pick up.

Enhanced Fujita Scale

In 1971 Dr. Tetsuya Theodore Fujita developed a scale for measuring tornado severity by wind speed. Fujita's scale was updated in 2007, becoming the Enhanced Fujita (EF) scale used today.

EF Number	3-second gust (mph)
0	65–85
1	86–110
2	111–135
3	136–165
4	166–200
5	more than 200

HAZARDOUS HURRICANES

Hurricanes are big, bold, and bad. These gigantic storms form in warm tropical ocean waters and gather strength as they barrel toward land. Hurricanes can be amazingly hard to predict. They can speed up or slow down as they approach, sometimes stalling for days. They can pound coastal cities with destructive winds, drenching rain, and a wall of seawater.

Before hurricanes had names, a massive hurricane smashed into Galveston Island, Texas, in 1900. A storm surge of 8 to 15 feet (2.4 to 4.6 m) covered the island. It was the worst weather disaster in U.S. history, killing at least 8,000 people.

In 1953 the U.S. Weather Bureau started naming hurricanes and tropical storms using an alphabetical list. At first storms had only women's names. In 1979 men's names were added. Could you share a name with a hurricane? Check the National Weather Service's web site for the hurricane name list. If your name starts with Q, U, X, Y or Z, don't bother looking. Hurricane names don't begin with those letters.

Some hurricanes are so destructive their names are retired and never used again. Terrible storms like Hazel in 1954, Camille in 1969, and Andrew in 1992 got those names retired.

Retired Hurricane Names

Between 2000 and 2010, 26 hurricane names have been retired.

2000—Keith

2001—Allison, Iris, Michelle

2002—Isidore, Lili

2003—Fabian, Isabel, Juan

2004—Charley, Frances, Ivan, Jeanne

2005—Dennis, Katrina, Rita, Stan, Wilma

2006—none retired

2007—Dean, Felix, Noel

2008—Gustav, Ike, Paloma

2009—none retired

2010—Igor, Tomas

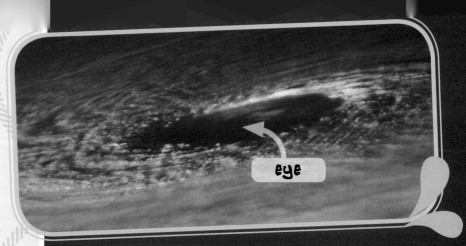

eye

At the center of even the wildest hurricane is a calm, quiet "eye" that can fool people into thinking the storm is over. But after the eye passes, pounding rain and howling winds slam back as fierce as ever.

Tornadoes and hurricanes often go hand-in-hand. In 2004 Hurricane Ivan caused a whopping 117 tornadoes in three days!

Hurricanes generally last only a few days once they hit land. But a storm very similar to a hurricane has been raging on Jupiter for at least 300 years!

On July 27, 1943, over the Gulf of Mexico, U.S. Colonel Joseph Duckworth twice flew his single-engine plane into the eye of a hurricane. He landed safely both times. Duckworth was the very first "hurricane hunter"—and he did it on a dare! Hurricane hunters have been monitoring hurricane conditions by plane ever since.

Saffir-Simpson Hurricane Scale

Herb Saffir and Bob Simpson developed the Saffir-Simpson scale in 1971. The scale uses wind speed to measure hurricane severity.

Category	Winds
One	74–95 mph
Two	96–110 mph
Three	111–130 mph
Four	131–155 mph
Five	greater than 155 mph

WEATHER
WEIRDNESS

Scientists who study weather track storms and predict what they might do next. Scientists can give warnings and safety advice. They can save lives with advances in weather technology. But nobody can be totally certain what weather will do next—and nobody can control it. Weather can be amazing, awesome, and absolutely bizarre.

Nature can shape snowballs without any human help. Wind can roll snow into large cylinders 2 feet (0.6 m) wide. To form, these snow rollers need gusty winds and temperatures just above freezing. A layer of ice needs to be on the ground, covered with a layer of new, fluffy snow.

The coldest recorded temperature in North America was on February 3, 1947. At Snag Airport in the Canadian Yukon, the temperature hit -81°F (-63°C). Spit froze before reaching the ground. Breath hung in the air like fog. Eyes watered and nose hairs froze. Brr!

In Baker, California, the world's largest thermometer towers 134 feet (41 m) high. Its height matches the hottest North American temperature, 134°F (57°C), which was set in 1913 in Death Valley, California.

Niagara Falls, the most powerful waterfall in North America, stopped on March 29, 1848. For hours, not a drop of water trickled over the falls because of an ice jam on the upper Niagara River.

In Phoenix, Arizona, the summer of 2011 was a bad season for dust! Monster dust storms struck three times, knocking out power, halting airline flights, and coating everything with dirt. Called haboobs, these gigantic walls of sand can be 50 miles (80 km) wide and more than 1 mile (1.61 km) high!

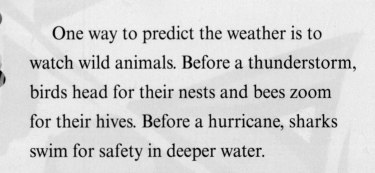

One way to predict the weather is to watch wild animals. Before a thunderstorm, birds head for their nests and bees zoom for their hives. Before a hurricane, sharks swim for safety in deeper water.

Pinecones are a good indicator of weather. On dry days pinecones open up wide to disperse seeds. On damp days pinecones close up tight.

Do you love lying out in the sun? Yuma, Arizona, is the place for you. It's nearly always sunny in Yuma—at least 90 percent of the time. It's the sunniest spot in the world!

Snow in June in New England. Lakes frozen in July and August in Pennsylvania. Widespread crop failures. It was 1816, the "year without a summer." All because a series of volcanic eruptions, ending with Mount Tambora in Indonesia, shot ash and dust into the sky. That volcanic debris brought global cooling and a snowy summer.

Hurricanes and tornadoes are known for their fierce winds. But strong winds don't always come with a storm. In December 2011 powerful winds blew through Southern California at gusts of 97 miles (156 km) per hour—equal to a Category 2 hurricane!

A massive drought hit the United States in the 1930s. Without rain, crops died. Without crops to hold the soil in place, soil turned dry and dusty. Wind lifted that dust into huge, billowing storms.

In 1932, 14 dust storms swept through the central states. By 1933, 38 huge dust storms struck. Farmland blew away—100 million acres (40 million hectares) of it!

April 14, 1935, called Black Sunday, brought the worst dust storms. Powerful "black blizzards" even reached New York and Washington, D.C.!

Now that you know about the world's weirdest weather, be prepared and aware. Learn what to do when wild weather strikes. Find the facts on weather safety, so you know what to do in case of tornadoes, floods, lightning, blizzards, and more. Be an expert who can outsmart the wildest weather whenever it shows up.

CHAPTER SEVEN

ASTOUNDING MILITARY TRIVIA

BEWARE THE PREDATOR

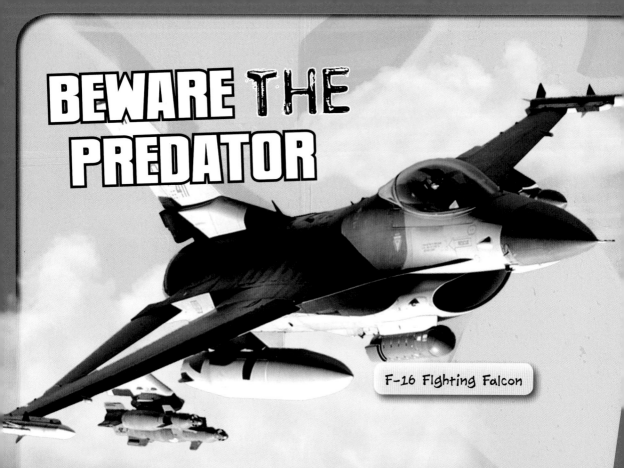

F-16 Fighting Falcon

What do falcons, ospreys, and seals have in common? If you said they're predators, you'd be right. And if you said they're all names of military aircraft or soldiers, you'd be right again. Uncover awesome facts about speedy F-16 Fighting Falcons, amazing V-22 Ospreys, and daring U.S. Navy SEALs. You'll also find out little-known facts about military battles of the past, the latest hi-tech military gear, and more.

V-22 Osprey

FEARLESS FIGHTERS

They jump out of planes and swim underwater. They trudge through swampland and sweat in the desert heat. Who are they? They're the fearless fighters of the U.S. military.

The Special Forces are some of the toughest, best-trained military troops. Members of these top forces learn unconventional warfare. While regular soldiers only learn to use three or four weapons, Special Forces weapons sergeants are skilled at using 80. They can assemble and use anything from an old-fashioned slingshot to a modern machine gun.

U.S. Navy SEALs are fit and fearless. They have to be to finish the fourth week of BUD/S training. They spend this week running, swimming, crawling, or paddling boats. They slog through obstacle courses and carry logs and inflatable boats. They do all this and more with only four hours of sleep in five days.

SEALs have unusual ways of getting around. They use amphibious assault crafts and mini-submarines. SEALs and their inflatable rafts can be dropped into water from a helicopter. SEALs call this a "rubber duck" entry.

What do U.S. soldiers eat when they're in combat? It's called a Meal, Ready-to-Eat (MRE). A soldier drops a pouch of prepared food into a special heating bag and adds water. Minutes later a hot meal is ready. Now that's fast food!

In 1960 U.S. Air Force Captain Joseph W. Kittinger, Jr. made a record-breaking jump. He jumped from a balloon 20 miles (32 km) above Earth to test out a new parachute system. Kittinger fell for nearly five minutes before his main parachute opened.

Sailors in the U.S. Navy speak their own language. They sleep in "racks" and shower in the "head." The wall is the "bulkhead" and the floor is the "deck." A "cranial" is a helmet and a "float coat" keeps them afloat if they fall overboard.

Cramming 6,000 crew members onto one ship doesn't leave much space for extra stuff. On Nimitz-class aircraft carriers, crew members sleep 60-to-a-room. Crew members have a storage bin under their bed and a locker the size of your school locker for their belongings.

They knew how to fly every kind of American military plane. But they were never allowed to fly them in combat. Women Airforce Service Pilots (WASP) trained male fighter pilots and flew other missions for the U.S. military during World War II (1939–1945). In 2010, nearly 66 years after the war, the WASP received Congressional gold medals for their service.

In 1995 U.S. Air Force Colonel Eileen Collins piloted a space shuttle. In 1999 she commanded the *Columbia* space shuttle. Colonel Collins is the first woman to pilot and command a space shuttle.

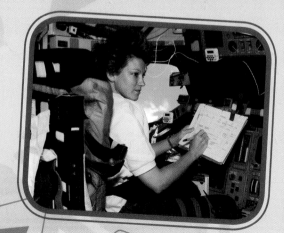

Today American military women do fly combat missions. Colonel Martha McSally was the first female Air Force pilot. In 1995 she became the first woman to fly a fighter jet in combat. In 2004 she became the first woman to command a fighter squadron. Colonel McSally flew more than 100 combat hours in an A-10 fighter jet.

Not all members of the military are human. Military working dogs are stationed around the world. Their keen noses sniff out bombs and drugs. Some dogs are trained to attack enemies. Some dogs even do parachute jumps with their handlers.

GETTING AROUND THE MILITARY WAY

Getting around is an adventure when you're in the military. From speedy jets and lumbering tanks to noisy helicopters and giant ships, each military vehicle has its own job to do.

The U.S. Air Force's Hurricane Hunters of the 53rd Weather Reconnaissance Squadron don't take shelter from hurricanes. Instead, they fly their Super Hercules airplanes right into the hearts of storms to gather weather data.

Nicknamed "the Warthog," the A-10 Thunderbolt II is thought to be an ugly airplane. Ugly or not, it's a mighty machine. The plane belches up to 3,900 armor-piercing shells per minute from its seven-barrel Gatling gun.

The Warthog has an armored cockpit made from titanium. This super-strong metal protects the pilot from armor-piercing shells. The cockpit's nickname is "the bathtub."

Have you ever seen a tank falling from the sky? Crews of the C-5 Galaxy have. The C-5 Galaxy is one of the biggest planes in the world. It carries tanks and drops them by parachute.

183

Aircraft carriers are the biggest warships in the world. The flight deck of the USS *Enterprise* is longer than three football fields. The carrier can store 60 planes with their wings folded up to save space.

Planes approach aircraft carrier runways at 200 miles (322 km) per hour. The pilot uses a hook on the plane's tail to grab a cable stretched across the flight deck. If the pilot misses and he or she can't take off again, the plane will end up in the ocean.

Aircraft carrier runways are short, so the planes need extra power for take off. Steam-powered catapults blast them into the air. A plane goes from 0 to 160 miles (257 km) per hour in three seconds.

In 1960 the nuclear submarine USS *Triton* finished the first underwater circumnavigation of Earth. It spent 60 days and 21 hours underwater.

The F-16 Fighting Falcon can fly at Mach 2. That's 1,500 miles (2,414 km) per hour, or twice the speed of sound. F-16s can withstand g-forces up to nine Gs. That's nine times the force of gravity!

Raptors are fast, stealthy birds of prey. The F-22 Raptor is a fast, stealthy fighter aircraft. Because of its shape and onboard technology, the F-22 is almost impossible to detect by radar.

A U.S. military rocket research plane called the X-15 was the fastest, highest-flying aircraft ever. In 1963 it flew an astonishing 67 miles (108 km) above Earth. Its record-breaking speed was more than 4,000 miles (6,437 km) per hour.

The CH 53-E Super Stallion is the U.S. military's biggest helicopter. It's so big it needs three engines and seven blades. It can carry 55 fully-equipped Marines or lift two Humvees off the ground.

The V-22 Osprey can hover like a helicopter and fly like a plane. Its enormous engines can be tilted up for vertical take off, or they can face forward for speedy flight.

The Stryker is an armored vehicle named after two U.S. soldiers who received the Medal of Honor. Private First Class Stuart Stryker was killed in World War II. Specialist Robert Stryker was killed in the Vietnam War (1959–1975).

British scientists think they have a way to make tanks disappear. It's called electronic camouflage. Pictures on the outside of the tank change to blend in with the tank's surroundings.

The Abrams tank is huge. It weighs about as much as 10 male African elephants. That could be why some people call it "the Beast."

Even the military wants to go green. The U.S. Navy is working on a plan to make fuel from pond scum, seaweed, and other types of algae. This new fuel has already been tested in a Seahawk helicopter.

WEAPONS AND GEAR

Weapons and gear are soldiers' tools—their lives depend upon them. Rifles, grenade launchers, and unmanned vehicles are just a few of the things that make up a military's arsenal.

What's the U.S. military's top gun? It's the M16 rifle. Almost all U.S. military members learn to fire it. Military forces around the world also use M16s. More than 8 million M16s have been used since their invention.

Soldiers have useful add-ons for their M16s. They can add laser pointers, night vision devices, or telescopic sights. An added-on M203 single-shot grenade launcher can blast away doors, windows, and bunkers.

Sniper weapons must be accurate over long distances. The XM2010 sniper rifle fits the bill. It has a range longer than 10 football fields.

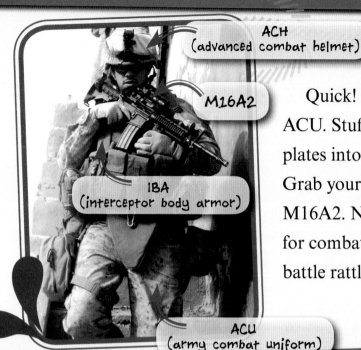

ACH
(advanced combat helmet)

M16A2

IBA
(interceptor body armor)

ACU
(army combat uniform)

Quick! Put on your ACU. Stuff your armored plates into your IBA. Grab your ACH and your M16A2. Now you're ready for combat in your "full battle rattle."

Scientists have found a way to help soldiers carry heavy loads over long distances. The HULC is a robotic exoskeleton. Wearing battery-powered titanium legs, a soldier can carry about 200 pounds (91 kilograms) of gear.

A fighter jet's sharp turns and fast dives create g-forces. G-forces push blood away from a pilot's head. Pilots wear special suits so they don't pass out. The suits squeeze their lower bodies to stop blood from collecting there.

"Spin 'N' Puke" sounds like a bad fairground ride. It's the nickname of a spinning machine used to teach pilots how to deal with g-forces.

This dog doesn't bark or beg for food. But it will be a soldier's best friend. The "BigDog" Legged Squad Support System carries up to 340 pounds (154 kg) of gear.

What flies without a pilot, spies without eyes, and shoots with pinpoint accuracy? It's the remote-controlled Predator. After a mission, the Predator is taken apart and easily moved to another location.

In the future, soldiers may skitter up walls like geckos. The Z-Man program has scientists studying animals to find a way for soldiers to climb without using ropes or ladders.

We'll take the FRIES today, please. The Fast Rope Insertion/Extraction System (FRIES) is a way to get soldiers on and off the ground in seconds. The soldiers attach themselves to a rope hanging from a helicopter. Then they either slide down or climb up the rope.

The tiny Nano Air Vehicle (NAV) is the size of a sparrow. Able to hover like a hummingbird, it someday may be used to spy on enemies.

MILITARY MIGHT OF THE PAST

War has existed as long as there have been people on Earth. From warriors shooting arrows to bombs dropped from planes, militaries have changed the course of history.

Dead animals as weapons? In the 1300s, militaries used catapults to launch rocks and sometimes rotting animals over castle walls. The attackers believed the rotting animals would spread disease to their enemies.

The first submarine to sink a warship was also the first submarine to be lost in battle. In 1864 the *H. L. Hunley* used the first-ever torpedo to sink an enemy ship. Then the *H. L. Hunley* sank and its crew drowned.

The 1st Minnesota Volunteer Infantry Regiment fought at the Battle of Gettysburg during the Civil War (1861–1865). When 215 of its 262 men were killed in one day, the regiment set a sad record. It was the highest casualty rate of the Civil War.

Almost 700 years ago, England and France fought the Hundred Years' War (1337–1453). English archers used bows that were as tall as the archers themselves. A good archer could shoot 10 to 12 armor-piercing arrows a minute from his longbow.

In World War I (1914–1918), German pilots fired machine guns bolted to their planes. They fired as they flew. The guns were timed to fire between the turning propeller blades.

The United States dropped the first atomic bomb ever used in a war. It was dropped on the Japanese city of Hiroshima on August 6, 1945, during World War II. It's thought that 80,000 people died immediately. Tens of thousands more died later from radiation poisoning or injury.

Poison gases were first used in World War I. Soldiers were given masks that filtered the air. If no mask was available, the soldiers were told to breathe through a rag soaked with urine.

The total number of deaths during World War I was 16,543,185. For each hour of the four-year war, 230 men died.

American Josephine Baker was a famous singer, actress, and dancer. And she was a spy! In World War II, she spied for France. Using invisible ink, she copied secrets onto sheets of music.

WHAT'S NEXT?

Both long ago and today, military troops and their weapons and vehicles have protected not only countries but also the people living there. What vehicles, weapons, and gear will militaries come up with next? We don't know—it's top secret!

CHAPTER EIGHT

CRAZY GROSS TRIVIA

GROSSER THAN GROSS

Some animals fling their poop. Some people use maggots to make cheese. People once even used pigeon droppings as hair dye. No matter where you look, people and animals do disgusting, gross things.

Most gross things are gross for a reason. Gross smells and tastes warn others to keep away. And it's usually best to avoid things that make our stomachs turn. However, we live in a strange world filled with all sorts of weird and wacky things. People from different parts of the world have different ideas of what's gross. If you think something is totally disgusting, someone somewhere might think it's beautiful or delicious.

Read on to learn about some of the grossest things on planet Earth. But be warned—you're sure to gag before you're done!

THE CRUDEST CRITTERS

Some critters seem to always be trying to gross us out. Some use poop in strange ways. Others eat animals from the inside out. These animals usually have good reasons for doing such gross things. But it may make you barf when you read about it!

When it feels threatened, the horned lizard squirts blood from its eyes. This gross action doesn't hurt the lizard. But it does send enemies running.

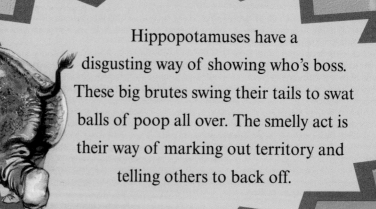

Hippopotamuses have a disgusting way of showing who's boss. These big brutes swing their tails to swat balls of poop all over. The smelly act is their way of marking out territory and telling others to back off.

Screwworm flies lay their eggs in the open wounds of warm-blooded animals. Many insects feed on the dead tissues of a wounded animal. But screwworm larvae eat living tissue. These maggots can actually eat an animal alive.

The kids will love this!

Dung beetles love poop! Some of these little bugs roll up tiny balls of poop for their future mates. Female beetles then lay their eggs inside the balls. The baby beetles eat the nutritious poop when they hatch.

The revolting hagfish has at least two disgusting behaviors. First, when threatened it produces big gobs of slime as protection against predators. It also has a gross way of eating. It grabs hold of a dead or dying fish and then bores a hole into its prey. It may also slither inside the fish's body through its mouth, gills, or rear end. Then the hagfish eats its victim from the inside out!

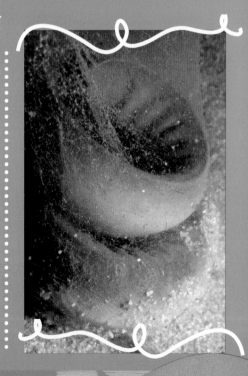

The pharaoh ant has a unique diet. It will eat regular ant foods like sugar and bread. But the tiny ant prefers meat and fat. It's been known to sneak into hospitals to dine on medical garbage. It seems to especially like blood and pus found in used bandages.

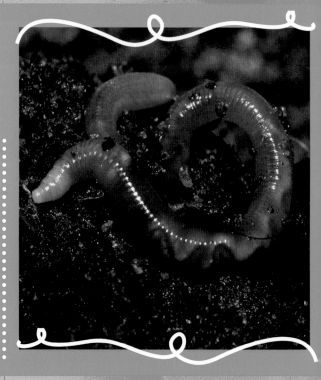

Earthworms have a disgusting way of eating. They "barf" their throats out of their mouths to grab their food. When they have a mouthful, the earthworms pull their throats back into their bodies.

Are they gone yet?

Opossums sometimes use a unique defense when they feel threatened. They fall over and poop so enemies think they're dead. It usually works. After all, who would want to eat a filthy, dead opossum?

Flies don't have teeth to chew their food like people. They vomit their digestive juices onto it instead. The fly barf turns the food into a soupy mess. Then the fly can suck the food up through its strawlike mouth parts.

A Pain in the Rear

OUTRAGEOUS
CRAZY GROSS
TRIVIA

Pinworms are tiny worms that can live inside your digestive system. Female worms wiggle down to your rear end to lay their eggs. At the same time, they release a chemical that causes intense itching. But scratching down there isn't a good idea. Pinworm eggs can get stuck beneath your fingernails. You could pass pinworms onto other people. People who have pinworms may even see the tiny critters come out in the toilet or in their underwear.

207

One of a face fly's favorite foods is snot! It loves the mucus that oozes out of a large animal's mouth, nose, and eyes. That's disgusting enough. But face flies also tend to spread eye diseases as they buzz from animal to animal.

Do you know why vultures are bald? Because it's not nearly as messy to shove a bald head into the body of a dead animal. Feathers would trap bits of rotting meat and blood on the vulture's head. The bloody mess could cause disease.

Let's eat!

Pass the ketchup!

The human botfly attaches its eggs to a mosquito or other blood-sucking insect. When the mosquito bites someone, the eggs drop off and hatch. Then the larvae crawl into the hole in the skin left behind by the mosquito. Inside the skin, the maggot feeds and grows until it's big enough to wiggle out and become a botfly. Botfly maggots often cause painful sores in a person's skin. They're usually not deadly—but they are super gross!

May the stinkiest dude win! Male lemurs have an odd way of finding a mate. They rub their bushy tails on smelly glands on their arms and chests. Then they wave their stinky tails at each other in a "stink fight." The lemur that stinks the worst usually wins the girl, and the loser runs away.

DISGUSTING DISHES

The saying goes, "You are what you eat." And from bugs to brains, it seems there's nothing some people won't eat.

Fried or roasted grasshoppers are a treat in some parts of the world. People in Thailand buy the crunchy critters by the bagful. They munch them like peanuts or popcorn!

In the Philippines some people dine on the brains of live monkeys! The animals are first given rice wine to make them drunk. Once they pass out, their skulls are cut open to have their brains scooped out. The practice is illegal. But some people continue to do it in the belief that it cures certain health problems.

People from Scotland sometimes eat haggis. The sausage-like meat is made from animal organs like sheep hearts, livers, and lungs. The meat is mixed with oatmeal, onions, and spices. Then it's stuffed into a casing of beef intestines to be cooked.

Vampires think blood is delicious. But they're not alone. Blood pudding, also called black pudding or blood sausage, is served in many parts of the world. The sausage is made with congealed animal blood mixed with oatmeal and spices. The blood for most pudding comes from pigs or sheep. Fans of blood pudding say it tastes like any other kind of sausage.

People sometimes eat the tongues of cows, which are very high in fat. Some cow tongue is even sold with the taste buds still attached!

In Sardinia people make a type of cheese called casu marzu. When the cheese is ready, flies are allowed to lay their eggs in it. Then the eggs hatch, and the maggots begin feeding on the cheese. Their digestive juices begin to decompose it. The process makes the cheese very soft, and it creates a flavor some people love. Eating half-digested cheese is gross enough. But that's not the worst part. The maggots tend to jump around a lot when you start cutting into the cheese!

In the United States, many people love eating hot dogs. But did you know that many hot dogs are made with animal "by-product"? This is a nicer way of saying "lungs, kidneys, and other parts." Many people don't realize they're eating ground-up animal parts they'd normally avoid.

People in several countries eat octopus. But in Japan and South Korea, it's considered a real treat. Living octopuses are sliced up so people can swallow the still wiggling tentacles.

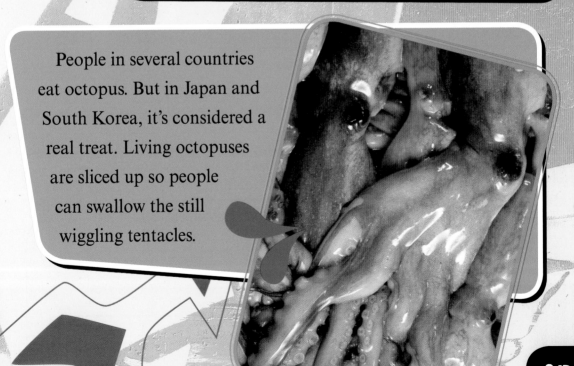

VILE TIMES

Hundreds of years ago, people were dirtier, sicker, and generally grosser than today. People didn't know much about germs back then. They didn't take a lot of care to keep things clean or use safe medical methods. These are just a few of the disgusting things people have done throughout history.

People didn't always have toilets available. Instead they pooped and peed in pots they kept in their homes. Each day they emptied the pots by dumping them out a window. They'd shout a warning to anyone passing by on the street below. The waste was then swept into the city's sewers.

Look out below!

Ever wonder why people shake with their right hands? Long ago people usually used their left hands to wipe themselves after going to the bathroom. So people used their "clean" right hands to greet others. Even today, greeting someone with your left hand is considered an insult in some countries!

Ancient Romans used some really gross stuff to color their hair. To make their hair lighter, ladies smeared pigeon poop and pee on it. To darken their hair, they used mashed-up dead leeches.

During the U.S. Civil War, soldiers used bat poop, or guano, to make gunpowder. The guano was used to produce nitrates. Nitrates are an important ingredient in gunpowder and explosives.

From about AD 400–1700, many people believed a surgery called trepanation was a cure for headaches. The treatment involved drilling a hole into the patient's skull. The hole supposedly released pressure on the brain, which would relieve the headaches.

Skulls of more ancient people have also been found with trepanation holes in them. It's thought that they believed the holes allowed evil spirits to escape a person's body.

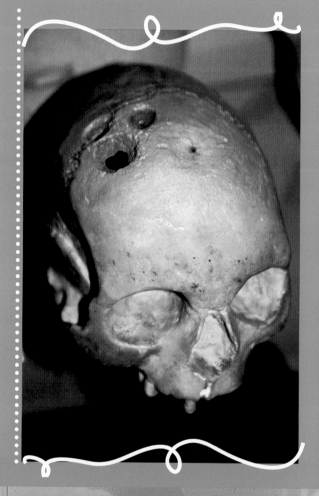

Belching after a good meal is considered good manners in some cultures. A big burp lets the cook know the food was satisfying. Tell that to your mom the next time you let one slip after dinner!

Did you have a shower this morning? Hundreds of years ago, you probably wouldn't have. Back then, people didn't bathe for months at a time, even for special occasions. The resulting body odor led to some traditions we still follow today. For example, brides started carrying flowers on their wedding days to hide their smelly body odor.

Most people know the ancient Egyptians made mummies. But did you know they pulled the dead person's brain through the nose with a hook? They didn't think the brain did much, so they simply threw it out. Meanwhile, most of the body's other organs were preserved in special jars.

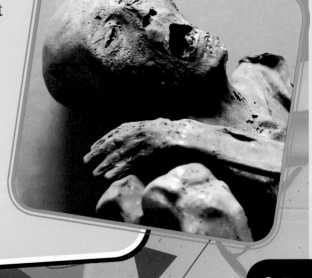

The black plague was a horrible disease that was greatly feared in the Middle Ages (about AD 400–1500). The plague first infected a person's lymph nodes. Victims developed huge lumps called buboes in their groin and armpits. The disease also caused high fevers, severe headaches, muscle pain, and blood vomiting. Tens of millions of people died from the disease in the Middle Ages.

Leprosy was once a disease feared by many people. The disease causes large, revolting sores on people's skin. Left untreated, leprosy can cause people to lose feeling in their hands, arms, and legs. Eventually these body parts become useless. It was once thought the disease caused body parts to decay and fall off. But this was found to be untrue.

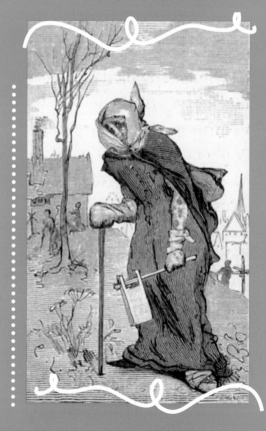

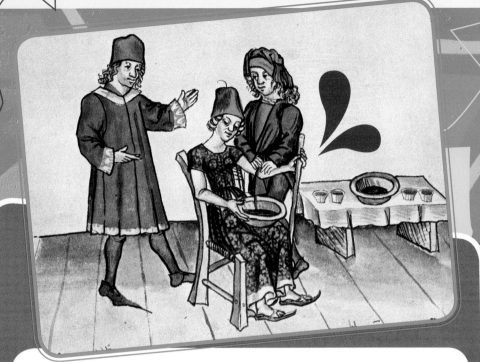

Long ago, people once believed that diseases were caused by too much blood in the body. Doctors often practiced bloodletting. They sliced open patients' arms and allowed their blood to pour out. The doctors thought less blood would return the patients to good health. However, this practice usually just made patients weaker and sicker. Sometimes they even died from the process.

The first public toilets were simply big pits in the ground. Everybody would do their duty in the same hole. To cover up the stink, they just threw some dirt on top of it. Unfortunately, the dirt didn't work too well. Most people found these public "privies" simply by following their nose.

YOU DISGUST ME!

Animals can be awfully disgusting. But there's something that can be considered even grosser—you! With boogers and barf and poop and pee, your own body is pretty gross too.

Everyone does it!

People's bodies are like factories. They are always working to keep people healthy and energetic. But like all factories, the human body is constantly producing waste. The average adult produces about 1/3 pound (0.15 kg) of poop and 1.5 quarts (1.4 l) of pee every day.

Did you know that dried-up earwax is always falling out of your ears? If you use earphones a lot, you probably have a lot of wax built up in there. Earphones can prevent the wax from drying up and falling out the way it should. So unplug and let the wax fly!

Your body constantly sheds old skin cells and makes new ones. Day and night, billions of dead skin cells fall off people and float around their homes. Dead skin cells actually make up most of the dust in your home.

Some people have tried drinking their own pee to avoid dehydration. But it's not a good idea. Your pee is full of salts and waste products that your body is trying to get rid of.

Your body is basically a big snot-making machine. Your mucous membranes constantly make snot that traps germs, dust, and other icky stuff. Although snot is useful, it's still gross. On average, people swallow about 1 quart (0.9 l) of snot every day!

A build-up of gas in your intestines causes farting. The gas comes from the breakdown of foods in your body. The average person passes about 0.5 quart (0.47 l) of gas a day. Farts stink because of a gas called hydrogen sulfide that is created as food is digested. Farts stink more if people eat foods that are rich in sulfur, such as beans or cabbage.

Eww, nasty!

Sweating helps keep your body cool. If that's the case, then your feet must be the coolest! Together your feet can produce 1 cup (240 ml) of sweat every day. People's feet are almost always covered by socks and shoes, which keep them warm. The sweat from feet can't evaporate and becomes trapped. No wonder a person's gym socks reek!

Everyone gets sweaty armpits sometimes. But did you know the sweatiest parts of the body may be the palms of your hands? Your hands have more sweat glands than any other part of the body. Good thing we wash our hands as much as we do!

You can't see them, but most people have tiny bugs called demodex mites living in their eyelashes. These little critters like to eat dead skin cells and the fluids from your eyes.

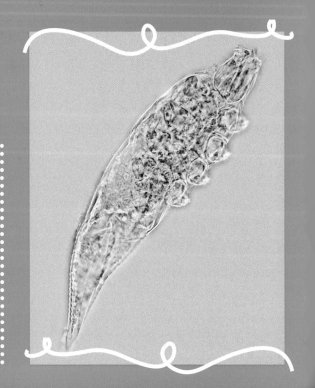

Picking your nose isn't just gross—it can also spread germs. Your nose produces plenty of snot that traps germs. When the snot dries out, it makes the boogers that you're tempted to pick out. But the germs are still there. You can spread those germs by digging in there and then touching other things. Be sure to blow your nose with a tissue instead.

Almost got it!

Zzzzzzz...

Ever wonder why your breath stinks in the morning? When you sleep, your spit doesn't flow much. Any bits of food left in your mouth don't get washed away. Rotting food just sits there all night, causing that horrible morning breath!

You've probably heard of a heart transplant. But have you heard about someone getting a poop transplant? The procedure is used for people suffering from severe digestive problems. Doctors first take a poop sample from a family member and process it. Then it's placed in the patient's stomach through a tube in the nose. The foreign poop contains healthy bacteria that help balance the patient's digestive system.

OUR DISGUSTING WORLD

Gross stuff can be found anywhere you look. It might lurk under a rock. It might be something an animal does. It may even be inside of you! But if you think something is disgusting, someone somewhere probably thinks differently.

It's OK to be totally grossed out by something you think is disgusting. Just remember—gross stuff has its place in the world too!

TRIVIA OVERLOAD!

Test your limits with this brain-busting match game.
Match the odds of probability to each unbelievable occurrence.

1. Odds of becoming President of the United States
2. Odds of becoming a pro athlete
3. Odds of making 3 hole-in-one shots in a row
4. Odds of a meteor landing on your house
5. Odds of having 20/20 vision
6. Odds of being injured by a toilet seat in your lifetime
7. Odds of living to 116 years of age
8. Odds of becoming famous enough to be mentioned in a history book
9. Odds of injury from using a chain saw
10. Odds you will die from a falling coconut
11. Odds of being bit by a poisonous snake
12. Odds of being an astronaut
13. Odds of being injured by fireworks
14. Odds of catching a ball at a major league baseball game
15. Odds of being born a twin in North America

A. 1 in 3
B. 1 in 4,464
C. 1 in 250 million
D. 1 in 563
E. 1 in 13.2 million
F. 1 in 10 million
G. 1 in 90
H. 1 in 19,556

I. 1 in 6,500
J. 1 in 156.25 million
K. 1 in 22,000
L. 1 in 6 million
M. 1 in 36 million
N. 1 in 2 billion
O. 1 in 182 trillion

ANSWERS

1-F, 2-K, 3-J, 4-O, 5-A, 6-I, 7-N, 8-L, 9-B,
10-C, 11-M, 12-E, 13-H, 14-D, 15-G

TRIVIA OVERLOAD!

Test your limits with this brain-busting match game.
Match each baby name to its adult animal species.

1. squab
2. calf
3. cheeper
4. kid
5. kit
6. hatchling
7. fawn
8. foal
9. infant
10. fledgling
11. pup
12. polyp
13. joey
14. shoat
15. owlet

A. beaver
B. deer
C. chimpanzee
D. kangaroo
E. partridge
F. goat
G. pigeon
H. eagle
I. whale
J. zebra
K. pig
L. jellyfish
M. owl
N. alligator
O. hamster

TRIVIA OVERLOAD!

Test your limits with this brain-busting match game.
Match the element with its symbol on the periodic table.

1. Oxygen
2. Sodium
3. Helium
4. Lead
5. Krypton
6. Copper
7. Potassium
8. Aluminum
9. Gold
10. Hydrogen
11. Radium
12. Silver
13. Tin
14. Iron
15. Platinum

A. O
B. Cu
C. Ra
D. Fe
E. Kr
F. Al
G. K
H. H
I. He
J. Au
K. Pt
L. Pb
M. Sn
N. Na
O. Ag

ANSWERS

1-A, 2-N, 3-I, 4-L, 5-E, 6-B, 7-G, 8-F, 9-J,
10-H, 11-C, 12-O, 13-M, 14-D, 15-K

TRIVIA OVERLOAD!

Test your limits with this brain-busting match game. Match each state nickname to its corresponding state.

1. The First State
2. The Sunflower State
3. The Pine Tree State
4. The Show-Me State
5. The Gem State
6. The Keystone State
7. The Pelican State
8. The Lone Star State
9. The North Star State
10. The Beaver State
11. The Badger State
12. The Silver State
13. The Granite State
14. The Golden State

A. California
B. Nevada
C. Minnesota
D. Missouri
E. Pennsylvania
F. Delaware
G. Wisconsin
H. Kansas
I. Idaho
J. Texas
K. Oregon
L. New Hampshire
M. Arkansas
N. Louisiana

ANSWERS

10-K, 11-G, 12-B, 13-L, 14-A
1-F, 2-H, 3-M, 4-D, 5-I, 6-E, 7-N, 8-J, 9-C,

TRIVIA OVERLOAD!

Test your limits with this brain-busting match game. Match each defunct team name with its respective sport.

1. Indianapolis Olympians
2. Brooklyn Bridegrooms
3. Muncie Flyers
4. New York Americans
5. Dayton Triangles
6. Montreal Expos
7. Tri-Cities Blackhawks
8. Minneapolis Red Jackets
9. Syracuse Nationals
10. Hartford Whalers
11. Quebec Bulldogs
12. Rochester Royals
13. California Golden Seals
14. Baltimore Bullets
15. Seattle Pilots
16. Chicago Orphans
17. Racine Tornadoes
18. Boston Beaneaters
19. Montreal Wanderers
20. Providence Steam Roller

A. National Basketball League (NBA)

B. Major League Baseball (MLB)

C. National Football League (NFL)

D. National Hockey League (NHL)

ANSWERS

1-A, 2-B, 3-C, 4-D, 5-C, 6-B, 7-A, 8-C, 9-A, 10-D, 11-D,
12-A, 13-D, 14-A, 15-B, 16-B, 17-C, 18-B, 19-D, 20-C

TRIVIA OVERLOAD!

Test your limits with this brain-busting match game. Match each (in)famous U.S. weather occurrence with its description.

1. The Tri-State Tornado
2. Hurricane Katrina
3. The Schoolchildren's Blizzard
4. Heat Wave of 1988
5. The Storm of the Century
6. The White Hurricane
7. The Armistice Day Blizzard
8. The Super Bowl Blizzard
9. The Galveston Hurricane

A. A November gale that whipped up waves as tall as three-story buildings lashed the Great Lakes on November 7, 1913. The great winds, snow, and rain resulted in more than 250 deaths.

B. A massive temperature drop and winter storm swept across the Dakota Territory and Nebraska on January 12, 1888, trapping many schoolchildren, in particular. It led to 235 deaths.

C. A weather quick-change caused temperatures to plummet and snowflakes to fly across the Midwest on November 10, 1940. The resulting 145 deaths included a number of duck hunters trapped by the freak snowstorm.

D. A low-pressure system caused rare wintertime tornadoes in the South before whirling into a giant snowstorm in the central Northern states. On the last day of the storm, January 12, 1975, the Minnesota Vikings (whose fans at home were being pelted by snow) lost the Super Bowl to the Pittsburgh Steelers, 16-6.

E. Some 700 people perished as the result of the deadliest twister in U.S. history on March 18, 1925. The tornado ravaged many communities and homes across Missouri, Indiana, and Illinois.

F. Up to 10,000 people perished from health complications due to heat in 1988. The heat wave was made all the worse by a drought before it that had its way with farmers and their rain-starved crops.

G. This Category 1 hurricane blew across the southern U.S. and particularly devastated the city of New Orleans, Louisiana, in 2005. The storm killed nearly 2,000 people and cost $125 billion in damages.

H. A popular tourist locale in Texas was nailed by a hurricane with estimated 135-miles-per-hour (217 kph) winds on September 8, 1900. The death toll was somewhere around 8,000 people.

I. A cyclone-blizzard that blew across 26 states claimed 310 human lives on March 12, 1993.

ANSWERS

1-E, 2-G, 3-B, 4-F, 5-I, 6-A, 7-C, 8-D, 9-H

TRIVIA OVERLOAD!

MILITARY

Test your limits with this brain-busting match game. Match each unique nickname with the corresponding U.S. war hero.

1. Boots
2. Old Hickory
3. Old Fuss and Feathers
4. The Swamp Fox
5. Rough and Ready
6. Ike
7. Uncle Billy
8. Black Jack
9. The King of Spades
10. Dugout Doug
11. Stormin' Norman
12. Stonewall
13. Unconditional Surrender
14. Ol' Blood and Guts
15. Black Death

A. Francis Marion, Revolutionary War
B. Thomas Jackson, U.S. Civil War
C. Andrew Jackson, War of 1812
D. Robert E. Lee, U.S. Civil War
E. Douglas MacArthur, World War II
F. John J. Pershing, World War I
G. Henry Lincoln Johnson, World War I
H. Frederick C. Blesse, Korean and Vietnam Wars
I. Dwight D. Eisenhower, World War II
J. Ulysses S. Grant, U.S. Civil War
K. George S. Patton, World War II
L. Zachary Taylor, Mexican-American War
M. Winfield Scott, War of 1812
N. Norman Schwarzkopf, Persian Gulf War
O. William Tecumseh Sherman, U.S. Civil War

1-H, 2-C, 3-M, 4-A, 5-L, 6-I, 7-O, 8-F, 9-D, 10-E, 11-N, 12-B, 13-J, 14-K, 15-G

TRIVIA OVERLOAD!

Test your limits with this brain-busting match game. Match each crazy gross (not to mention embarrassing) nickname with the name of its animal parent.

1. Shaglet
2. Spat
3. Eyass
4. Hoglet
5. Polliwog
6. Nymph
7. Pupa

8. Elver
9. Whelp
10. Wriggler
11. Fry
12. Flapper
13. Fingerling

A. Stinkbug
B. Frog
C. Butterfly
D. Eel
E. Octopus
F. Otter
G. Fish

H. Oyster
I. Hedgehog
J. Swan
K. Mosquito
L. Cormorant
M. Falcon

ANSWERS

1-L, 2-H, 3-M, 4-I, 5-B, 6-A, 7-C, 8-D, 9-F,
10-K, 11-E, 12-J, 13-G

IMAGE CREDITS

dedMazay, 31 (b), Denis Barbulat, 37 (t), Denis Vrublevski, 71 (m), Dennis Donohue, 59 (b), Dietmar Hoepfl, 151 (m), 183 (ml), discpicture, 223 (t), Djordje Radivojevic, 13 (b), Dmitrijs Dmitrijevs, 23 (b), Dmitriy Shironosov, 81 (m), Domenic Gareri, 131 (t), Doremi, 183 (mr), Dr. Morley Read, 35, DVARG, 68 (t), Eclipse Digital, 27 (b), 153 (ml), Edwin Verin, 51 (t), ehammer, 136 (tr), ekler, 131 (b), elmm, 137 (b), Eray Arpaci, 120 (b), Eric Isselée, 6 (br), erwinwira11, 181 (m), Eugene Buchko, 22, feathercollector, 43 (t), Fejas, 136 (t), Fer Gregory, 29 (t), Fernando Cortes, graffiti illustration used as background, Florida Stock, 64 (t), 105 (b), Four Oaks, 7 (b), 205 (t), Frantisek Czanner, 196, Galyna Andrushko, 66 (b), 157 (t), George P. Choma, 25 (bl), happydancing, 147 (t), Harper, 130 (b), hd connelly, 83 (b), Henrik Larsson, 24 (t), Hhsu, 107 (t), HitToon.com, 28 (m), Hugh Lansdown, 44 (t), Igor Chaikovskiy, 85 (ml), Igrik, 17 (m), ilFede, 220, indiwarm, 74 (l), iofoto, 135 (b), Jan Kowalski, 223 (b), Janne Hämäläinen, 67 (b), jannoon028, 81 (b), Jiri Vaclavek, 26 (tr), Joellen L. Armstrong, 152 (m), John T. Takai, 103 (br), Julien Tromeur, 25 (green germ), JustASC, 77 (t), 163, Kacso Sandor, 80 (b), kaktuzoid, 25 (blue germ), Kamira, 14, kapu, 20 (t), Kathathep, 9 (no smoking sign), Ken Durden, 132 (t), Kesu, 23 (t), Klara Viskova, 169 (m), kornilov007, 19 (b), ktsdesign, 46 (m), kurt_G, 56 (b), lafoto, 151 (b), Laura Gangi Pond, 29 (b), Laurence Gough, 63, 87, lavitrei, 155 (b), Leonidtit, 147 (m), LilKar, 40 (b), lineartestpilot, 215 (bl), 225 (b), Liusa, 27 (m), Lynx Aqua, 189 (b), Map Resources, 21 (br), Marcel Clemens, cover, 71 (drops of Mercury), Marco Mayer, 113 (b), Marie C. Fields, 71 (t), Mariette Budel, 39, Maximus256, cover, 90 (U.S. Map), Melanie Metz, 158, Michael Lynch, 36, Miguel Angel Salinas, 179 (t), mikeledray, 206 (b), Mikhail Popov, 142 (t), mirabile, 194 (b), mmutlu, 79 (b), Molodec, 21 (m), Morten Degn, 17 (t), mountainpix, 52 (t), Nathalie Speliers Ufermann, 54, Neilras, 30 (b), nenadv, 81 (t), Nick Stubbs, 143, Nip, 38 (t), Oguz Aral, 9 (lungs), Oleksiy Mark, 73 (m), Olena Pivnenko, 212 (t), Olga Donskaya, 225 (t), Olga Miltsova, 72 (b), olly, 86 (b), Om-elchenko, 64 (m), Paul Cowan, 211 (t), paulvg, cover, 1, 2 (brain), Pete Niesen, 119, Phase4Photography, 27 (t), Photofish, 48 (m), Piko72, 90 (l), Pushkin, 146, Rachael Grazias, 104, Rafael Pacheco, cover, 85 (moon), Sam Dcruz, 208 (b), Sapik, 140 (b), Sari O'Neal, 52 (b), Sashkin, 29 (m), 153 (b), Scott T. Slattery, 35 (snail), Seamartini graphics, 19 (m), Sebastian Kaulitzki, 79 (t), Sebastian Tomus, 159 (m), serazetdinov, 46, (fish shoal), 76 (b), Sergej Khakimullin, 147 (b), Sergey Mikhaylov, 204 (b), Sergio Hayashi, 93 (b), Sferdon, 216 (b), sima, 153 (t), Stephen Coburn, 8 (l), Steve Cukrov, 138 (b), Steyno&Stitch, 177 (b), Studio Barcelona, 148 (b), Studio37, 217 (b), Susan Flashman, 42 (r), SvitalskyBros, 209 (b), Symbiot, cover, 24 (m), (spider), Takeiteasy Art, 134 (t), Tena Rebernjak, 15 (b), titelio, back cover, 129 (ball), Todd Shoemake, 19 (t), Tony Oshlick, 222 (t), Tootles, 221 (b), Tribalium, 6-7, 11 (fireworks), 219 (b), TyBy, 153 (mr), unkreativ, 73 (b), untung, 8 (ri), 23 (snake), Vava Vladimir Jovanovic, 213 (t), Ventura, 139 (b), vicspacewalker, 65 (t), Vinicius Tupinamba, 206 (t), vitek12, 69 (t), Walter G. Arce, 136 (m), Yobro10, 129 (br), YorkBerlin, 51 (bl), yuri4u80, 69 (b), Zastol'skiy Victor Leonidovich, 170 (b), Zeljko Radojko, 76 (t), zentilla, 70 (m); STScI/NASA/R. Beebe, A. Simon (NMSU), 165; Tim Tevebaugh, 166; U.S. Air Force photo, 178 (b), 181 (t), 187 (t), Airman 1st Class Benjamin Wiseman, 183 (t), Master Stg. Kevin J. Gruenwald, 186 (b), Roland Balik, 183 (b), Staff Sgt. Lee O. Tucker, 174, 186 (t), Tech Sgt. James Pritchett, 182, Tech Sgt. Erik Gudmundson, 194 (t), TSGT Ken Hammond, 190; U.S. Army photo, 176, Jason Kaye, 188 (b), Sgt. Grant Matthes, 191 (b); U.S. Department of Health and Human Services CDC, 80 (t); U.S. Marine Corps photo, 191 (t), 178 (t), Jennifer J. Pirante, 193 (t), Lance Cpl. Joseph M. Peterson, 192 (t); U.S. Navy Photo: Mass Communication Specialist 2nd Class Brian Morales, 185 (t), Mass Communication Specialist 2nd Class John P. Curtis, 179 (b), Mass Communication Specialist 2nd Class Joshua T. Rodriguez, 195 (t), Mass Communication Specialist 2nd Class Kyle D. Gahlau, 177 (t), Mass Communication Specialist 3rd Class Scott Pittman, 175 (t), 184 (b), 188 (t), Mass Communication Specialist 3rd Class Shonna L. Cunningham, 184 (t), Mass Communication Specialist Seaman Chad R. Erdmann,187 (b), Photographer's Mate 1st Class Ted Banks,189 (m), Photographer's Mate 2nd Class Katrina Beeler, 181 (b); U.S. Navy SEAL and SWCC photo, 175 (b); University of Chicago, 161 (b); Visuals Unlimited/David Phillips, 221 (m); Weldon Owen Publishing: Dr. Mark A. Garlick, artist, 169 (b); Wikimedia/Stubb, 65 (b); Wikipedia/Russell and Sydney Poore, 149 (b), Zylornian, 204 (t); Yesterday's Classics/The Baldwin Online Children's Literature Project, www.mainlesson.com, 110 (b)

INDEX